STEVE **MARTORANO**

YO CUZ!

MY LIFE. MY FOOD. MY WAY.

BY STEVE **MARTORANO**

WITH MICHAEL **RUBINO** AND CHIP **SILVERMAN**

This is how
it started
with a menu
on a
"Blackboard"
18 years ago.
Yo Cuz!

FOREWORDS BY FRANK **VINCENT + LUDACRIS**

A SPECIAL MESSAGE FROM CUZ **GEORGE**

INTRODUCTION BY JOSEPH R. **GANNASCOLI**

NORTHSTAR MEDIA

Published by Northstar Books
Recipes by Steve Martorano

Library of Congress Catalog-in-
Publication Data available.

ISBN: 978-0-9819802-6-3

Manufactured in the USA

10 9 8 7 6 5 4 3 2

Northstar Media, LLC
120 East Vermont Street
Indianapolis, IN 46204

www.northstarmediabooks.com
www.cafemartorano.com

FROM STEVE MARTORANO

My Recipes Have Evolved From Inside Of Me.

If you are buying my book as a 'paint by numbers' way to learn great Italian-American cooking, you will be greatly disappointed.

I will tell you what ingredients I use, but I will never hold your hand and show you how much of this or how little of that.

If I did, you would never understand not only what I do, but also how and why I do it!

When I cook, I feel such intense love and joy for my family, friends and all those during my lifetime who have deeply appreciated what I do.

And when I cook I also feel the pain and sorrow and loss for those in my life who are gone.

I cook as a tribute to my family and all whom I have loved and who have loved me.

I cook to honor the passion and love they cooked into our family meals.

I cook for my Mother, whom I'm so blessed to still have and who I know is proud of me.

I cook when I'm happy and when I'm sad.

I cook with my all my heart and with my soul.

How the fuck can I turn these feelings and emotions into ingredients in the pages of my book?!

Well, I can't and I won't!

If this book will teach you anything, it is to feel your food, to experiment with the flavors, herbs and tastes and learn to do what you do when cooking with your emotions.

And then, and only then, you will understand who I am and what I do.

And when you come to one of my restaurants, you will know why you let me do what I do and don't break balls!

-Steve Martorano
YO CUZ!

Inside this book:

I don't want to offend anyone, but I curse. Right or wrong, it is what it is. This is my life, this is how I grew up, and these stories are about the people and places that have made me what I am today.

DO YOU KNOW THE DIFFERENCE BETWEEN 'SAUCE' AND 'GRAVY'?

WHAT THEY'RE SAYING

"The food, the music, the atmosphere…second to none. Steve is simply the best and always gives back to the community, you never have to ask him twice."
Jason Taylor, Miami Dolphins

"Steve, you cooked me my favorite and it was the best I ever ate in my life. I tell the world. Thanks for all the great times."
Fat Joe, musical artist

"I've never seen Jimmy so excited about a guest. I guess Steve blew him away, because Jimmy invited him back to his home to cook for everyone. Personally I've never eaten better in my life."
Uncle Frank from the Jimmy Kimmel Show

"The best Bucatini Carbonara I've ever had! Steve is a genius in the culinary world."
Tom Cruise, actor

"Steve, incredible food, vibe, fun, spirit! Great experience!"
Jamie Foxx, musical artist/actor

"Your food is so good it warms the soul. There is always a smile and good times at Café Martorano, my favorite! It's the first place I bring all my friends."
Chris Carter, former NFL Great and Hall of Famer

"Best food in Florida. Always celebrate my birthdays at Café M. Much love and success to my Cuz Steve. Virgos rule!"
Ludacris, musical artist

"Great food, great music, great people."
Peyton Manning, Indianapolis Colts, Super Bowl Champion

"Café Martorano's is the best Italian in America."
Rene Angelil, manager and husband of Celine Dion

"One word to describe it is AMAZING! Steve, you always have my love!"
Gabrielle Union, actress

"This is by far the best in the world."
Chazz Palminteri, actor, "The Bronx Tail," "The Sopranos"

"Steve is the best cook ever."
Lorraine Brocco, actress, "The Sopranos"

"I have always been a huge fan of the Martorano experience! Whenever I go to Steve's place, I enjoy some of the best food of my life and then end up dancing on tables…not to mention his meatballs are epic! What else could you ask for?"
Mario Barth, celebrity tattoo artist

"I initially felt that Steve would be an interesting guest for my show, as Chefs are very popular these days. Little did I know the impact this man had on my audience and me. This tattooed tough guy with the softest heart rocked us all with the most inspiring story of passion, hope, risk and tenacity. This modern day example of the 'American Dream' is an inspiration to us all."
Monique, actress and comedian, "The Monique Show"

"What a terrific place. Thanks Steve."
Paul Sorvino, actor

"Great eats. The best."
James Caan, actor

"The guy does not make mistakes so I'm proud to meet his creations. You're a great man with many talents. Life is everything and your food is real."
Ray Lewis, Baltimore Ravens

"Amazing evening. The food, music and movies are unbelieveable."
Kenneth "Baby Face" Evans, recording artist, producer and song writer

"This is the best ever, Steve even cooks a great steak, this is my home."
Dan Marino, Miami Dolphins NFL Hall of Famer

"The best I ever had."
David Proval, Richie Aprile on "The Sopranos"

"The best food in Vegas, period!"
Sugar Shane Mosley, boxer

"Steve & Crew: off da hook! Service and food, one of da best!"
Guy Fieri, cook, TV personality

"Thanks for letting me do the Michael Jackson Dance at your incredible place."
Chris Tucker, actor and comedian

"The only thing I like better than your food is my horses."
Joe Pesci, actor

"You need a place in London!"
Tom Jones, musical artist

"Steve Martorano - pound for pound one of the hardest knocking chefs around, his passion for cooking is exceeded only by his love of music."
Joseph R. Gannascoli, actor, chef, author

"You'll laugh...You'll cry...Mostly you'll get hungry... Now sit down and eat. Kudos, Cuz."
Frank Vincent

"Steve Martorano has created the most amazing atmosphere and the highest quality of food I have ever experienced in the restaurant business."
Jim Allen, Chairman, Seminole Hard Rock Entertainment

"My wife and I love Steve's food so much we used to drive an hour from Boca (Boca Raton, Florida) almost every night, often getting there too late for the first seating. So after years of this and having to wait to eat, we decided to move right around the corner from Café Martorano. Now we eat there at 5:30 every night. Heaven!"
Earnie Maresca, song writer, "Run Around Sue"

"This cookbook that Stevie has written with his recipes is as soulful and real as the music that I played for the past 51 years. Like his food, it comes from the heart not a research chart! Long live Steve Martorano! Sincerely, 'The Geator with the Heator, The Boss with the Hot Sauce.'"
Jerry Blavat, world famous DJ

"Steve is a brilliant perfectionist, obsessed, passionate, uncompromising man. A true genius!"
-Douge Fresh, record producer

"Last night I watched in amazement this man, Steve Martorano, simultaneously cooking, spinning records, playing movies, greeting guests and orchestrating the finest restaurant on this planet. No one else I know can do this!"
DJ Irie

"Even with all his fame and notoriety, Steve, more than anyone I know, appreciates and acknowledges his roots. His humble, sincere nature is impressive!"
Sylvester Stalone, actor

"I've been going to Stevie's joint since he opened 20 years ago. I've never had a bad meal, a bad attitude or a bad time. I always leave happier than I came. (Steve must have that formula locked up somewhere.)"
Mitch Grossman

"This man has a natural born talent to make people feel good."
Bon Frosch

"The best meatball I have ever had and don't forget the pastini & butter! You need to come back on when you book is done!"
Jimmy Kimmel, TV Personality

MARTORANO ACKNOWLEGEMENTS

"It's not how hard you hit. It's how hard you get hit and keep moving. That's the difference between a winner and a loser." These are words that I have lived by for the past few years that have helped me to keep moving and get this book done.

Over the years I have met a lot of people have pushed me and urged me to write this book, to put my heart and life down on paper. Most of all, they wanted my fucking recipes. So here it is.

This book is a testament to perseverance, commitment and belief in myself. There were a lot of people who said I couldn't and I wouldn't do it. There were and still are a lot of people that hope and wish that whatever I do I fail. This book is My Life, My Food, My Way.

To everyone in my life who is represented in this book, I thank you for giving me life experiences that helped me to be who I am today. To all my family and friends who have believed in me and continue to encourage me, I love you and thank you.

How long until you meet someone who puts you first and them last?

How long, not long.

How long until you meet someone who doesn't yes you when everyone else does?

How long until you meet someone who lifts you up when your down?

How long not long.

You changed my life forever! Marrrrrrrr Aka Mush

Love you and respect you and admire you.

Yo Cuzzzzz!

Look Ma... I did it!
Yo Cuzzzzz

TABLE OF CONTENTS

MARTORANO

FRANKIE VINCENT

The first time I met Steve Martorano was at his Fort Lauderdale restaurant, Martorano's. I was invited to dinner there with a couple of fellow "Sopranos" actors and I couldn't believe the food! It was better than any restaurant I have ever eaten in. That evening also had extra touches that knocked me off my feet!

To begin with, the walls had photos of many great actors, including Sinatra, Martin, Brando and cast members of "The Sopranos." Not bad company! Music was being played by Steve himself, as he cooked and DJ'd at the same time. However, the highlight of the evening was when he played scenes from favorite movies on the TV monitors. When it came to a scene that one of us was in, Steve would lower the music, dim the lights and turn up the volume of the monitors. The restaurant guests would then applaud. It was like having dinner in front of an audience – ingenious!

Steve Martorano is without a doubt one of the most creative and passionate people I have ever met. He comes from a background of love and respect for family and tradition, and it comes through in his desire to please. After reading this book, you'll have the strong urge to visit one of his three great restaurants. When you walk in, just mention my name and make sure you order the meatballs, which are the best in the world. Steve's recipe for meatballs, among so many other dishes, is pure heaven. NOW, SIT DOWN AND EAT!

Much love cuz,
Frankie Vincent

LUDACRIS

"My Favorite restaurant, hands down.

It's where you get an unforgettable experience of a lifetime. I'm going to rename Martoranos as "the 5 senses," because it's the only place where it stimulates all of your senses. Your sense of hearing because of the music, sight because of the TV screens and all the visuals, smell because of the aromas coming from the kitchen, of course taste because of the outstanding food, and touch because you feel the love of family and friends all around you. Again, no other restaurant can compare."

"I dream my painting and then I paint my dream."
-Ludacris

COUSIN GEORGE

Bright is the night that I pin this sitdown of words. Dimmed is the light, for I write before a high narrow prison window. Below me is the city of Philadelphia. The city that created the two of us. My beloved cousin Steven and, I, George.

The streets and the intriguing culture. The family that raised us was of two things: hard and full of flavor. Hard because the streets took my life away. Flavor, that brought my cousin to the heights of where he is today. Great resturants, great gravies and great wines.

Although we both grew up hard on those backstreets, the criminal thoroughfares eventually brought us to that fork in the road. My cousin, being reared in a household of great foods and lifelong lingering aromas, chose the road of spices and atmosphere. I took the sad avenue of broken lights where I could not see the dead end.

In time, time took command of us both. The years passed. Steven struggled to make a positive name for himself, of which I am truly proud. In time, I began to understand the four walls of my cell and learn to express myself as a writer. Yet, there isn't a day that goes by that I do not remember the smells and taste of the wonderful working man's food that was on our table in those early years of our ethnic heritage.

Today the name Martorano is known far and wide, both from my cousin Steve's success and extraordinary taste buds and, on the other hand, from my accomplishments buried in the fourth world, prison.

This book of stories and food, I believe, is the first of its kind. Never will a mixture of family and flavors present itself as the moving pages of this very different cook book. Not only are you reading about great ingredients, you're also reading about a well-talked-about family and its history, a history made up of strong character and amazing plates of food.

-George Martorano
12973-004

1914

JOSEPH R. GANNASCOLI

It's pretty cool that I get to write this intro for Stevie.

He has been a friend now for quite some time. I myself have cooked and been around so many kitchens in so many cities I've lost count; New York, New Orleans, Los Angeles, New Jersey, Boston, Chicago and so on and so forth. I have met many, many Chefs here and in Europe, but none is as cool as Stevie. He's hip, he's cool. He could've cooked for Sinatra, McQueen, Dean—they would have dug him. He loves what he does and loves to watch people enjoy it. All the great ones do. I used to love watching plates come back to my kitchen empty and demand to know why when they weren't. Now you throw in him spinning great music and great visuals, i.e., movies, TV shows and celebs paying homage, presto you have a slamming restaurant.

Now you know why there is a 4 1/2 hour wait to get in, with big shots, actors, ball players and the hottest girls. When the other side of midnight comes, the lights get dimmer, the music gets louder and the fun goes deep into the morning. But make no mistake about it, it's not all fun and games. Stevie cooks one way: HIS WAY, and no booze, you gotta run down the block for a pop, (which I have, many times during the night!!) or you could enjoy his wine list, which has the most wine in South Florida. Did I mention the restaurant seats 80? Amazing, right? If you haven't been there yet, make it a destination trip, it's worth it. Just don't ask for something that's not on the menu or to change something or to complain about the wait. You might find yourself in a jackpot or, worse yet, getting "the look" from my cugine, Steve Martorano.

-Joseph R. Gannascoli

CAFÉ MARTORANO

MARTORANO

Steve Martorano didn't start out as a gleam in his father's eye so much as he did a rumbling in his mother's stomach. While pregnant, the lady craved pasta seven days a week. Make that macaroni, not pasta—we're talking about South Philly, after all. In retrospect, it was little surprise that her only child would create three of this country's most innovative Italian-American restaurants: Café Martorano in Fort Lauderdale, Martorano's at the Rio in Las Vegas and the newly opened Martorano's Italian-American Kitchen at the Hard Rock Casino in Hollywood, Florida.

Specializing in taking South Philly-style food to the next level, Martorano reinterprets old-school Italian-American classics from The Neighborhood and serves them with a side dish of popular culture; the touchstones of film, television and music. If you're lucky, not only will Martorano make you his famous meatball with to-die-for Sunday gravy, the former club DJ will climb back into the booth and spin classic disco, soulful R&B and, of course, Sinatra. Whether through the food or entertainment, an evening at Café Martorano delivers an autobiographical tour of this cook extraordinaire's life and successes. "I'm not a chef," he says.

Here, though, are the details (and recipes)—the good stuff: always direct, sometimes disturbing and utterly South Philly. These stories will send you from the family table to the mean streets to a row home basement, the place where the son of a part-time loan shark took one of Philadelphia's most notorious names and made it into its most delicious.

Serving the World Famous
Martorano Meatballs in gravy.

PROLOGUE MARTORANO

After we heard what happened, on March 15, 1981, Fat Frankie had to see it for himself. As we were ordering cheesesteaks, two guys ran by us yelling, "They just blew up Phil Testa's house." I wanted my cheesesteak first. We threw down the money at Oregon Steaks and drove to Girard Estates in South Philly, getting there before the fucking cops and ambulance, but arriving in time to do nothing but watch in disbelief.

By then, a crowd had gathered in the cold on the dark street in front of the neighborhood's nicest home. People running. People standing. People sitting on the curb. They were in a daze, the whole neighborhood—crying and whispering. Speculations of what happened made the rounds through the crowd.

"His house—it just exploded. But it was only his house; he's OK."

"You're full of shit, jerk-off. He's dead. They killed him."

"No, he's alive—burnt the fuck up, though."

It was March, but smelled like the Fourth of July. Steam rose off metal bits that covered the ground. Soon the scene was flooded with lights from the police cars and paddy wagons. Parts of Testa, some of his clothes and his personal belongings, were scattered all over the park across the street.

When we saw what was left of Philip Testa, the whispering turned into screaming.

Testa was the boss of the Philly mob, a close family friend, and father to my friend Salvie. The former boss, Angelo Bruno, had been assassinated by some of his own men almost a year earlier, in March of 1980. Now it was Testa's turn. After a short period of uncertainty, he was picked by The Commission to head the Philly mob from a group of men that included my Uncle Raymond. Testa or Uncle Raymond, it made no difference to Salvie and me, two guys in their early 20s bouncing around South Philly from corner to corner. Whoever got picked, we were going to be able to walk the neighborhood with respect.

Then the shit hit the fan. We were used to violence in South Philly, but nothing like this.

"What the fuck is happening in Philly?" someone cried.

Jesus Christ, I thought, another boss? Was this a message from the Irish mob—a big "fuck you" for the problem with their roofers' union? Who would kill a boss unless it was sanctioned by New York? Testa was just made the head of the Philadelphia family. Killing Testa made it two bosses dead in less than a year.

I sat on the curb and unwrapped my cheesesteak, still warm but soggy.

What the fuck is happening, I wondered, and who the fuck is next? My uncle? There wasn't going to be any house on the hill for a guy like him, that was for sure. In his line of work, you didn't retire—it was either life in prison or you got whacked. If I followed in that path, how was I going to avoid the same fate?

I took a bite of my cheesesteak and watched the craziness in front of me. I didn't know it at the time, but the answer was in my hand.

Steve Martorano with one of his three dogs, "Dino," named after Dean Martin.

Home-style Philly Cheesesteak

Where does a guy start? Aside from Oregon Steaks, you've got Geno's, Pat's, Tony Luke's, Steve's up in northeast Philly, and Jim's on South Street. I loved all of those places, but my mother made the best.

>>> My mom got some top of the round meat and had the butcher slice it thin. She'd put a little bit of extra-virgin olive oil, a tablespoon of butter and sliced white onion into a pan then seasoned it with a litte Kosher salt and crushed black pepper. She'd cook the onion slowly until it got brown. In a saute pan she'd warm extra-virgin olive oil, and after it was heated she'd add the steak. When it started cooking she'd pull it apart until it was cooked all the way through and then she'd season the meat with Kosher salt and crushed black pepper and add the cooked onions then put slices of American cheese on top, and cover the pan. When the cheese starts melting, mix everything together, then stuff it into your favorite crisp Italian bread. Add sliced cherry peppers and that is South Philly all the way.

Philly Pizza Steak

>>> Sometimes my mother would make her famous pizza steak. It's pretty much the same as a cheesesteak but she'd add sliced beefsteak tomatoes that were marinated in extra-virgin olive oil, Kosher salt, crushed black pepper, fresh oregano and fresh basil. She'd add sliced marinated tomatoes on top of the meat and then the cheese. *Yo Cuz. That's a Taste of Philly!*

Top: Steve Martorano, working out at the Zoo gym Fort Lauderdale.

Middle: Fresh veal stock, simmering overnight for 24 hours.

Bottom: Chef Ariel Benitiez making Sunday Gravy.

GRINO

Yo Cuz

07-11
YO CUZ1
FT. LAUDERDALE
47

Yo Cuz

SECTION 1

Food, Family and Philly

Steve's (2) Great-grandmothers and his Grandmother and Grandfather

THE UNITED STATES OF AMERICA

TO BE GIVEN TO THE PERSON NATURALIZED.

No 2280197

CERTIFICATE OF NATURALIZATION

Volume Number 401-M

Description of holder: Age, 19 years; height, 5 feet, 6 inches; color, white; complexion, ruddy; color of eyes, brown; color of hair, black

Visible distinguishing marks, none

Name, age and place of residence of wife none

(NOTE:—AFTER SEPTEMBER 22, 1922, HUSBAND'S NATURALIZATION DOES NOT MAKE WIFE A CITIZEN.)

Names, ages and places of residence of minor children none

ORIGINAL

George Martorano (Signature of holder)

The United States of America, Southern District of Texas ss:

Be it remembered, that GEORGE MARTORANO then residing at number Troop K, 4th Cavalry Street, McAllen, of Texas who previous to his naturalization was a subject of Italy having applied to be admitted a citizen of the United States of America pursuant to law, and at a regular term of the District Court of The United States held at Brownsville, Texas on the 10th day of May in the year of our Lord nineteen hundred and 21 the court having found that the petitioner intends to reside permanently in the United States and that he had in all respects complied with the Naturalization Laws of the United States, and that he was entitled to be so admitted, it was thereupon ordered, by the said court that he be admitted as a citizen of the United States of America.

In testimony whereof the seal of said court is hereunto affixed on the 1st day of June in the year of our Lord nineteen hundred and 26, and of our Independence the one hundred and Fiftieth year.

(SEAL)

L. C. Masterson, Clerk.

U.S.Dist.Court, S.D.T. (Official character of attestor)

By [signature] Deputy.

DEPARTMENT OF LABOR

The document: Steve's grandfather's, George Martorano's, Immigration Certificate when he came to the United States from Sicily.

CHAPTER 01

I am an Italian kid— I am an Italian guy from South Philly, with no education and no formal culinary skills, who used to sell chicken cutlet sandwiches with broccoli rabe out of my mom's tiny basement. Probably didn't seem like much at the time, but I had a dream and followed it. I didn't listen to nobody but myself, didn't let no one or nothing stand in my way.

Twenty-five years later, my place in South Florida, Café Martorano, is one of the most successful restaurants around. There's another Martorano's at the Rio in Vegas that's been going gangbusters for almost 3 years, and we just opened Martorano's Italian-American Kitchen at the Seminole Hard Rock Hotel and Casino in Hollywood, Florida. Not too long ago I was on the late-night show "Jimmy Kimmel Live!" teaching America how to make my famous homemade meatballs and Sunday gravy.

After we did the show, Kimmel asked me to stay in LA a couple of extra days to cook at his home for his friends and family and to watch Sunday football. Guess who stopped by to eat? Tom Cruise and his mom. He wanted bucatini carbonara, which he had just eaten while visiting Italy. I must have done pretty well. Before I was able to leave the kitchen to join the others, Tom's mom came in holding an empty plate. "Look," she said, smiling proudly. "I had to tell him you can't eat the dish."

Bucatini Carbonara. You won't know what hit you.

Bucatini Carbonara

This is the Italian-American version. I use heavy cream, but in Italy they don't.

Tom Cruise didn't know what hit him the night I cooked my version for him at Jimmy Kimmel's house.

>>> Melt a tablespoon of butter. Add a handful of diced panchetta (Italian bacon). You can get this at your Italian market. First, render the panchetta until it's crispy. Then, add a cup and a half of heavy whipping cream to the pan and let it reduce by half. Taste for salt, add crushed black pepper and a handful of Parmigiano-Reggiano cheese. Mix together very well.

>>> Now that the sauce is done, cook the Bucatini (or you can use spaghetti) in lightly salted water.

>>>Whisk two raw egg yolks in a bowl, drain the al dente Bucatini and add to the egg yolks. Then add the cream mixture to the Bucatini and egg yolks.

>>>Add more crushed black pepper and cheese to taste. Mix together extremely well like a salad. Plate it and add an egg yolk on top.

Café Martorano Meatball (Martorano's Famous Meatball)

"May be the best meatball in the world."
-Gourmet Magazine

>>> For meatballs, use 1 pound each of veal, beef and pork and mix them together (sometimes your butcher will mix them together for you). Crack two large eggs into a bowl and whisk them together. Pour the eggs into the meat mixture. Add crushed black pepper, Kosher salt, granulated garlic powder, 2 cups of finely chopped fresh Italian parsley, 2 cups of Parmigiano-Reggiano cheese and 1 cup of Italian-style Progresso bread crumbs.

>>> Get a loaf of day-old Italian bread and break it into small pieces. Soak the bread in warm water until it's soft, then squeeze all the water out. Really squeeze all the water out! Add the bread to the meat mixture and mix everything together.

>>> Roll a 4-ounce ball or whatever size you like. One of my grandmothers made hers big, the other one made hers small.

>>> Fill a deep pan half way with vegetable oil and make sure the oil is hot before adding the meatballs. To test the oil, take a small piece of meat from a meatball and throw it in the oil. If the meat begins to fry, it's ready to go.

>>> Working in batches, brown the meatballs for 3 minutes on one side and then 3 minutes on the other side. This is the secret to a great fucking meatball.

There's nothing better in the world than waking up on Sunday morning and eating a fried meatball for breakfast. So let's keep this Italian tradition going.

> It's important to NEVER put your meatballs in marinara sauce. You need a Sunday Gravy because that's what puts it over the top. The sausage, the pork, the pigs' feet, the pigs' skin, the braciole—that's what makes the package work.

Me? Cooking for celebrities? That kind of shit doesn't happen to a guy who grew up on Sunday Gravy.

Yo, Cuz, it ain't sauce, it's gravy. We didn't have sauce in my neighborhood. Get it straight. And it's not pasta, we call it macaroni.

Where I grew up, on a Sunday morning, fuck the alarm clock, you didn't need it—we had fried meatballs. You would wake up after staying out late on a Saturday night, maybe still even had a little buzz, and—oh, shit!—it would hit you. You'd hear the meat sizzling. Smell the tomatoes with the garlic, olive oil and the pork. Forget about eating bacon and eggs in our house. Hangover or not, you wanted to get your ass out of bed to get to that plate of fried meatballs and slap a few on some soft, white American bread with mayo or gravy. Yeah, mayo—that's the American side of me.

My mom made a pot of gravy on Sundays that consisted of pigs' feet, pigs' skin, ribs, sausage, braciole and especially meatballs. Some people baked their meatballs, some people threw them right into the pot, but we fried ours first. Before the meatballs went into the pot, we'd tear through a dozen or so of them. My mother would always yell, "Stop, there won't be any left for dinner," so I'd make a gravy sandwich: sliced bread, gravy, grated cheese. Simplicity is always the best.

Dave Algor rolling The World Famous Martorano Meatballs

South Philly Sunday Pork Gravy

"It's not sauce, Cuz, it's Gravy." Now break out the shopping list, cuz. You're gonna need it. This is enough to feed the entire crew.

>>> You'll need: 5 pounds of pork butt, cut into half-inch pieces; a pound of sweet Italian sausage; a piece of fat back, cut into quarter-inch pieces; six pigs' feet cut in half; three pieces of pork skin: 15 cloves fresh garlic; fresh basil; Kosher salt; crushed black pepper; extra-virgin olive oil; and eight to 10 cans of San Marzano tomatoes.

>>> Add a quarter cup of extra-virgin olive oil to a pot or Dutch oven. TIP: If you get your pan extremely hot then add the cold oil, your food will never stick.

>>> When the oil is hot (not smoking) add the pork butt pieces and let them begin to brown. Season them with Kosher salt, crushed black pepper and granulated garlic. Brown on all sides, which takes about 10 minutes. Remove the pork butt and repeat the same steps with the sausage. Add the beef or pork braciole or both. After the braciole has browned, remove it from the pan, then add the fat back pieces to the pan and brown them as well. Add 15 cloves of smashed garlic. Let the garlic brown. Put the tomatoes in a clean bowl and crush by hand. Then add the tomatoes to the fat back and garlic and bring the sauce to a rapid boil. Season with Kosher salt and crushed black pepper and lower the heat to a slow simmer. Add all of the cooked meat and simmer for about 2 hours (not all day).

>>> A few tips from a guy from South Philly

> You don't need to add sugar because you are using a great quality canned tomato.

> Do not add red wine (leave that part for "The Godfather").

> If you are also making meatballs, add a few tablespoons of the oil you fried the meatballs in to the gravy.

> 15 minutes before you add your meatballs to the gravy, add a few handfuls of grated Pecorino Romano cheese and lots of fresh basil. Then put your meatballs in.

George Martorano, aka "The Gink," enjoying himself New Years Eve 1950s... You think he had too much to drink?

All the row homes on our street smelled like mine with that delicious aroma of Italian tradition. Everyone who lived there was Italian, or at least it seemed like that to me. We might have had a couple of Irish families here or there, and basically you said your hellos and goodbyes, but that was it. The blacks lived in the projects down the street, but none of us ever went in there; we heard that if you went in, you never came back out. It was a black-white thing. Back when I was growing up, Martin Luther King Jr. was assassinated, and our parents took us out of school early fearing a race riot. Growing up in South Philly, there was always tension between the blacks and whites, especially during the summer. When I think about it today, it's really kind of funny. Neighbors would set their beach chairs in the front yard to watch us yell and throw bottles at each other.

I attended an all-white grade school, but as I got older, times changed. In the eighth grade a black girl joined our class, and by the time I was in high school, I made friends with a lot of black kids. One day I brought a black kid named "Cheesy" to my home for lunch. Everyone watched and stared as we walked through the neighborhood to my house. When we got to my front door my mother was waiting and simply asked what we wanted for lunch. She welcomed my guest with open arms and, of course, great food.

The Italian-Americans I knew based everything on food. Someone got married, there was food. Someone died, there was food. You didn't feel good, there was food. They fed you and fed you and fed you. The only way you got skinny was if you went to prison. It was like Weight Watchers or something.

Grandmom frying meatballs.

Steve making meatballs.

CHAPTER 02

Among my friends and neighbors, the weekly menu was a ritual that never changed despite the weather or the season.

Every Monday your mother made a pot of soup, like chicken or ox tail. On Tuesday and Thursday, we had the leftover gravy from Sunday with a different cut of macaroni (Rigatoni tasted different than fusilli. Fusilli tasted different than perciatelli). Wednesdays she did chicken or veal cutlets with ketchup on the side, chicken-flavored Rice-a-Roni and a salad. On Friday, it was linguini and clams, peppers and eggs, or tuna fish salad with hard-boiled eggs and sliced tomato. Never any meat, it was a Catholic thing. Saturday your mom didn't cook—it was her day off. Saturday was always pizza (which we called a tomato pie) from the local Italian bakeries, cheesesteaks or cold cuts.

Gram's house, 767 S. 6th Street. Everyone just chillin!

Veal Insalata

This dish, like so many of the others, was inspired by my mother's cooking. Wednesday nights we always had veal or chicken cutlets with Rice-a-Roni and a crisp salad on the side. If you're making this dish, don't forget the Rice-a-Roni.

>>> Start with a few medallions of veal, either the top of the round or the tenderloin (we use the tenderloin, but it's a bit costly). You can get your butcher to slice them thin or pound them yourself. Season the medallions of veal with Kosher salt, crushed black pepper and a little granulated garlic powder. For the next step you're going to need flour, eggs, bread crumbs and three clean bowls. In the first bowl put flour, in the second bowl crack four large eggs. Season the eggs with Kosher salt, crushed black pepper, Italian parsley and 2 tablespoons of Parmigiano-Reggiano cheese, and whisk the mixture together. In the third bowl put bread crumbs.

>>> Working one medallion of veal at a time, place the medallion of veal in the flour and cover lightly, then dip it in the egg wash and lastly in the bread crumbs. When all the medallions are finished, let them rest in the refrigerator for an hour or so.

>>> In the meantime, put together a Martorano salad. In a bowl, combine 2 cups of chopped romaine lettuce and some cucumber, red onion and tomato. Season with Kosher salt, crushed black pepper, granulated garlic, extra-virgin olive oil and imported red wine vinegar to taste. Add freshly grated Parmigiano-Reggiano cheese and toss lightly.

>>> After an hour, fill a pan a quarter full with olive oil and heat it. When the oil is hot, fry the cutlets over medium heat. Get them nice and brown on both sides. When all cutlets are done, plate with the Martorano salad and serve.

But Sundays were the best. On Sunday in South Philly you always heard someone say, "What time do you want me to put the water on?" This referred to the water used to cook the macaroni. Rigatoni was my favorite. Every Sunday, my mother would make rigatoni and keep the leftovers in the refrigerator. Late at night I'd go downstairs, take out the bowl of macaroni, pour a glass of homemade iced tea, watch some TV, and then head back to bed. Even cold macaroni right out of the refrigerator was delicious; that's how you knew your mother was a great cook.

My father's mother, Mary, did a lot of cursing. Everything she said was fuck. When I was a little boy she watched me while my mom worked, so I guess I came by it honestly, right? I know the first word out of my mouth—even before Ma or Da—had to be fuck. Fuck this, fuck that. It's just what she said, the way she talked. "Go get me a pack of fucking cigarettes." "Go get me a fucking beach chair." "Go put the fucking pot of water on." When I was young it seemed like everybody went to her house on Sundays. Everybody: neighbors, family, and their kids, and somehow there was always enough food. There was always a feast—a fucking feast.

Gram was old-school Italian. She was born here in America and my grandfather came from It-lee (Italy).

They had a big family: four sons—Raymond, Joe, John and Anthony—and two daughters—Angie and Phyllis. Gram never worked, but she always had money; nobody ever understood how or why. She kept it hidden in her bra. You needed money? You'd go to Gram and she'd reach into her bra and peel out the cash—$5, $10, $20. Then she'd whisper, "Don't fucking tell nobody."

Gram always sang to me. My first Italian-American song I learned was "I Have But One Heart." She called me her *pishadel*, which means little bird. When I'd stay the night with my grandmother, my aunt used to find me asleep with a bowl of cold macaroni in my lap with the TV on in the background. It got so bad with me eating, I had to sleep with my Aunt Angie. She would put the bureau in front of the door so I couldn't get out of bed to go down to the kitchen. Guess that was the first time I got locked up.

Gram made homemade ravioli, spaghetti and the best ricotta gnocchi. We usually ate Sunday dinner at 5:00 p.m., but by 8 o'clock Gram would call me into the kitchen and bring out two jars of pickled pigs' feet that my grandfather made. I'd climb into her lap and Gram would feed me pickled pigs' feet, and we'd put ketchup on them. Her love and food kept our family together.

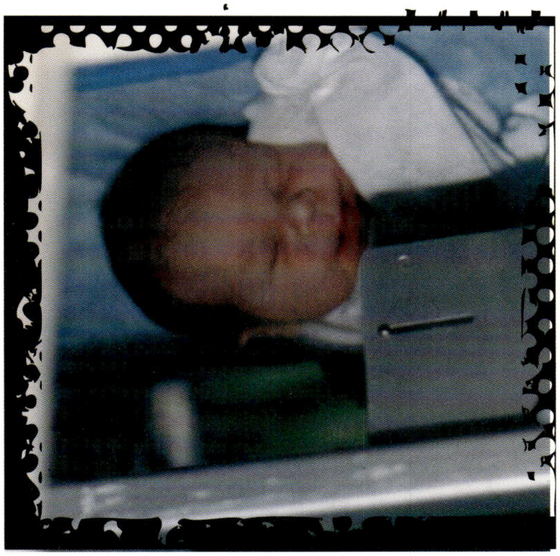

Top: Steve with his Grandmother at 767 South Fitzwater Street.

Bottom: First born Son, Joey, in an incubator, fighting for his life—The Martorano Way!

The Gink's Wild Mushroom Saute

My Grandfather Martorano, whom my grandmother called "The Gink," was a great cook. Back in the day, he'd go mushroom hunting, then come home and make this appetizer, which we either ate on crusty Italian bread or alone with bread crumbs. You probably don't go mushroom hunting, but you can get the same results with a combination of Oyster, Portabella, Shitaake and Button mushrooms. Or, if you want to do just one kind, knock yourself out—it'll still be great.

>>> Work in batches if you have to. Saute four cloves of smashed garlic in extra-virgin olive oil. Once the garlic is browned, add crushed red pepper flakes. Then add the mushrooms and saute for about 8 to 10 minutes over medium heat. Season mushrooms with Kosher salt, crushed black pepper, granulated garlic and coarsely chopped fresh Italian parsley. Let cook until mushrooms are soft. Add some homemade toasted bread crumbs and more fresh Italian parsley. This dish should be dry, not wet.

Top: Aunt Philly and Grand Uncle George

Middle: My grandmother Mary, Etta, Grand Pop George and me at the renewal of their vows after 50 years of marriage. I'm their Best Man.

Bottom: My Grandfather, Anthony Durante, aka "The Wolf." A bad motherfucker.

My grandfather on my mother's side, Anthony Durante, died before I was born. They said he was a tough son of a bitch. His nickname was "The Wolf." I remember my mother telling me that my grandfather shot somebody in the neighborhood because this guy took a piss in front of my mother and her family as they were taking a walk. My grandfather got furious, took his family back home, got his gun, and left the house. He didn't come back for a week. In the meantime, my grandmother heard about a guy being shot the night my grandfather disappeared, and she figured my grandfather was hiding out until things cooled down. I remember as a kid seeing an old man limping in my neighborhood. My ma told me that was the guy my grandfather shot.

My ma's mother, Sue Durante, who I called Nanny, lived with us. Nanny was widowed at an early age, left to raise my mom and her two brothers, Tony and Louie. Compared to Gram, Nanny was more of a modern grandmother. She worked, shopped and loved to play bingo. On the side, she took numbers on Saturdays. Neighbors and friends—maybe 20 or 30 people—would call the house with their bets. A quarter bet could score you $100. It was a good way to make a little extra cash in the neighborhood. But eventually the government figured that out, made it illegal, and started their own lotteries.

Like her mother, my mother was a modern woman for her time, and worked in a place that manufactured bathing suits. Lillian Martorano was beautiful—fairly tall for an Italian woman (5-foot-7 or so) with reddish-blonde hair, and always looked sharp and well dressed. She was the kind of woman who, when she walked into a room, people wanted to know who she was. Because my Grandfather Durante died when she was young, my mom worked pretty much all of her life and gave her paycheck to her mother. But even though she worked a lot, my mother still knew how to cook a helluva meal.

We didn't have a whole lot of money, so some of her best dishes were her most basic. One of my favorites was pastina with Breakstone's whipped butter, a dish I serve to this day. In the wintertime, when it was really cold, we'd watch TV (our favorite shows were "The Honeymooners" and "Sanford and Son") and eat "Italian soul food." My mother took that great American standby, the hot dog, and cut it up along with bell peppers and onions. Hot dogs and peppers was peasant food, but we felt like the rich eating filet mignon.

Pastini and Butter

This dish is so simple that when I give it away in the restaurant, people come over and ask, "What was that delicious specialty?"

"Pastina and butter," I tell them. "You gave it to your kids when they were babies."

>>> Cook the pastina in lightly salted water. Grab yourself a bowl and add some lightly salted butter (preferably Breakstones). When the pastina is finished add to the butter, with a few tablespoons of the macaroni water. Then mix the pastina and butter together and add freshly grated Parmigiano-Reggiano cheese. You can add crushed red pepper flakes at the end if you want to.

This is simplicity at its best!

Hot Dog and Peppers

This one is so good that on a cold day, it'll make your dick hard.

This is what I cooked on "The Monique Show" in Februrary, 2011.

>>> Get a pack of all beef hot dogs and slice the hot dogs on an angle into one-inch pieces. Heat your frying pan and add extra-virgin olive oil to the pan. When the oil is hot, add 3 cloves of smashed garlic and brown. Then add one sliced white onion and season with Kosher salt, crushed black pepper and granulated garlic. Cook until tender. Then slice two bell peppers, add to the pan and cook until tender. Then add the chopped hot dogs and cook over medium heat for about 15 minutes. Next, add a can of imported San Marzano tomatoes and season with Kosher salt, crushed black pepper and fresh basil. Let cook for about 20 minutes. Optional: add a handful of Parmigiano-Reggiano cheese. You can serve this in a bowl or in crisp Italian bread as a sandwich.

My father, Joe Martorano, was thin until he got married and then he got heavy—5-foot-10, about 250 pounds. He did whatever he had to do to make a buck, keep a roof over our heads, and put food on the table. He wasn't a fancy guy—didn't care for cars, clothes or a big house—but loyal as hell and respected. He taught me that relationships were very important in life. As long as things were good with his family, he was a very happy guy who loved to joke around. He also did some loan sharking, and when I bought my first car I borrowed money from him. I had to pay it back, plus the points to teach me responsibility. When I was a little older, he ran a bar/restaurant in South Philly called Anton's on 11th and Ellsworth.

His primary job, though, was at John's Vending, the biggest business of its kind in Philadelphia. Two of his brothers, John and Raymond, owned the place, and the rest of the family worked there. My cousin Carol, Aunt Philly's daughter, helped run the company. She was like the sister that I never had. Very loyal! Now she's the one who helps keep this family together, just like my grandmother once did. They supplied cigarettes, cigarette machines, pinball machines and jukeboxes all across the state and in parts of New Jersey. I grew up loving music because my father would bring home 45s from the jukeboxes, mostly R&B and Motown stuff.

It was a family business, but one of vending company's most interesting employees ran a different kind of "family" enterprise.

Philadelphia mob boss Angelo Bruno was, at one point, a salesman for the company. During his reign (1959-1980), the Philly mob grew in notoriety, making Bruno one of the top Mafia leaders in the U.S. Some said his old-world ways caused him missed opportunities in narcotics and in Las Vegas. But he always maintained close ties with New York. And, more importantly, he was able to gain control over the emerging gambling empire of Atlantic City. Nicknamed the "Docile Don" or "Gentle Don," there was very little violence during his reign.

Angelo Bruno was a very close friend of my Uncle Raymond, the oldest of my father's brothers. If you saw Angelo walking in the neighborhood, my uncle was stride for stride with him. If Angelo crawled, Uncle Raymond was right there, too. Like my father, Uncle Raymond was a heavy-set guy. Then he went "away" in the late 1950s and got thin and remained that way.

Top: Steve and his friend Anthony at The Mansion, Wildwood N.J., at a Sunday afternoon beach party.

Right: Steve's father at Atlantic City.

CHAPTER 03

To me, he was just Uncle Raymond, but in the headlines it was always Raymond "Long John" Martorano.

Legend had it, he got the nickname when he was a kid because he always wore long-john underwear under his clothes.

Of course, my cousins and I didn't have the balls to call him "Long John"—at least not to his face—and in return he never called us by our names. It was always, "Howya doin', kid?" or "How's my nephew?" That kind of shit made me nervous, but as a kid it was about all you were going to get out of him. When Uncle Raymond was around, you were on your best behavior.

But more often than not, it seemed like Uncle Raymond wasn't around.

When he went away to prison, we only saw him when he requested to see us. My cousins or I would smuggle peppers and eggs and chicken-cutlet sandwiches into the joint, stuffing the food in our socks and down our pants so we wouldn't get caught. If you got caught, they took the food and you lost your visiting privileges. He'd always ask about our families, and then take us aside individually for one-on-one talks.

Peppers and Eggs

Everyone needs to know how to make this, because what are you going to eat when you wake up at about 2 o'clock in the morning and you've got nothing in the house?

>>> Cut a bell pepper into strips and fry them in extra-virgin olive oil. Season with Kosher salt and crushed black pepper. Beat and season 6 eggs with chopped Italian parsley, Kosher salt, crushed black pepper and grated Parmigiano-Reggiano cheese. When the peppers are soft, add the egg mixture and scramble together. Put that on some crisp Italian bread and you'll think you've died and gone to heaven.

Top row left to right: Uncle Johnny, Grand Pop, Uncle Anthony and a family friend Johnny DeMarco.

Bottom left to right: Aunt Terri, my mother Lillian, Aunt Angie, Aunt Eta and Aunt Philly.

Once, when I was visiting my Uncle Raymond in prison, he told me the story of "The Scorpion And The Turtle." It went like this: There was a scorpion and a turtle that lived near a river. One day the river was rising and threatened to flood the riverbank and drown the scorpion. The scorpion asked the turtle for a favor. "Please," he said, "let me hop on the back of your shell and take me to the other side of the river." The turtle said no, fearing the scorpion would sting and kill him. "I give you my word," said the scorpion, "I won't sting you." The turtle agreed, and the pair made their way to the other side of the river. However, when they made land, the scorpion stung the turtle. Shocked and disappointed, the turtle asked why the scorpion had gone back on his word. "I am what I am," said the scorpion.

I loved that story because it taught me to look out for myself, that there are people who have it in their nature to take advantage of you. Scorpion? Turtle? I didn't want to be either one, but in South Philly there weren't a lot of other options. Plus, whatever I did, I wanted my family to be as proud of me as they were of Uncle Raymond.

When he got out of prison, Uncle Raymond was always busy on the streets turning the Martorano name into something honorable. In our neighborhood, if you needed something you went to him. Couldn't pay the electric bill? Go see Raymond. Young guys in the neighborhood getting too big for their balls? Raymond. Trouble with the boss at work? You guessed it. Uncle Raymond knew everybody, and everybody knew him. He was respected, but also feared.

When I was 17, on one of my aunts' birthdays, Uncle Raymond took our family to The Latin Casino across the river in Cherry Hill, New Jersey, to see Frank Sinatra perform. What a treat! I was raised on Sinatra (years later, even got a tattoo of Ol' Blue Eyes when he died in 1998). As a kid, I learned all his songs by listening to a couple of local radio shows called "Friday with Frank" and "Sunday with Sinatra" hosted by a DJ named Sid Mark.

When I became a teenager and everyone had long hair and was listening to The Who and The Rolling Stones, I remained a die-hard Sinatra man. On Sundays, my buddies would come over and we'd drive down to the lake in Philadelphia where we washed and waxed our cars. We wore white wife-beater T-shirts and black slacks and kept our hair nice and short. And as we cleaned our car and cruised for girls, we'd blast "Sunday with Sinatra" from the car radios. When we'd come home, my mother would leave out a bowl of fried meatballs for us. We made fried meatball sandwiches and listened to Sinatra.

Meatballs and Sinatra was a religious experience, but to see him in person with Uncle Raymond took things to a whole new level. When Sinatra came on stage that night at the Latin Casino, he walked over to our front-row table, greeted the entire Martorano family, and then extended his hand to my aunt. As an Italian-American, it was like getting a blessing from Jesus Christ. And being around Uncle Raymond was like spending time with the pope.

The Raymond Martorano I knew was a far cry from the kid who got his balls busted for wearing long johns. All of the kids—especially his son George and me—wanted to be on the street and just like him because of his standing in the neighborhood. He dressed sharp and commanded people's attention but was low-key. He didn't want to bring attention to himself. He didn't need to; everyone knew Raymond Martorano was one of the wealthiest and most respected men in South Philly. He wasn't one to fuck with.

My Frank Sinatra tattoo. I never had the pleasure of meeting him in person, but as far as I'm concerned, he's always a part of the Italian-American tradition.

CHAPTER 04

As the son of a guy who worked in the vending machine business, my pockets didn't bulge with a wad of cash like Raymond's. They jingled. My allowance and school tuition was paid in change: quarters, dimes and nickels. I admired my parents for working hard, but having real money—a roll of bills—was all that mattered to me. Money was power, but in our house money was tight.

Despite my parents' financial circumstances, they never complained, especially my father. Joe Martorano was a guy who seemed to never get a break in life. He worked in the vending business, and even though it was a family operation, my father usually got the short end of the stick. His brothers Raymond and John ran the place while my father and his other brother Anthony did the labor part of the work. "Joe, deliver these cigarettes." "Deliver this jukebox." Do this, do that—that kind of shit. But that's what family did back then: they helped each other, they were loyal, and, even if they didn't like something, they kept their mouths shut.

When gambling was legalized in Atlantic City, my father began renting a van and charging guys to drive them to the Resorts Casino. He wasn't a gambler or drinker, so while his crew spent all their money in the casino and got drunk, my father would walk around or stand with his hands behind his back waiting for them. Then, after the guys had lost all their money, they'd hit him up for loans—a couple of hundred bucks here and there. Eventually, instead of waiting around for hours, he started selling nylons and pantyhose to the cocktail waitresses out of the van. Three for a dollar, four for a dollar, whatever he had to do to make a buck, that's what my father did. I respected him for that.

Otherwise, everything he got were seconds, hand-me-downs from his brothers. Once, he drove home in a white Cadillac. His big new car was really Uncle John's old one. But my father didn't care. It was new to him and to us. In the mid-1970s, when I was in high school, my father had an opportunity to be head of the bartenders union in Atlantic City—a dream job arranged by Uncle Raymond. But before he even started, Angelo Bruno and Uncle Raymond took it away: It wouldn't look good to the feds, they decided, if there were too many Martoranos running things.

My father never said a word, showing only love and respect. In private, I could tell it hurt my father and mother—but I knew it was business.

My grandmother, her two sisters and their husbands in Atlantic City.

CHAPTER 05

My mother and father always stressed the importance of a good education, but I was never cut out for school. The nuns at King of Peace elementary on 26th and Wharton didn't show much interest in me. Maybe it was because I didn't show much interest in learning. All my friends had nicknames like "Weasel," "Fish," and "Petey Pump." Mine was "Stevie Truck," because my father drove a delivery truck for a living. I guess everyone figured I'd be doing the same one day. Fuck them.

By the sixth grade, I stopped giving a shit thanks to a particularly miserable nun who probably just needed to get laid. Once, she sent me home with a report card with all Fs. On the way home that Friday—with the whole weekend in front of me—I decided to take a pen and turn the Fs into Bs. What was I thinking?

"What's this?" my mother asked.

"My report card."

"I know what it is," she said, "but the grades?"

My father shook his head. "All Bs?" he said. "Something's not right?"

I stuck by that story the whole weekend. But on Monday, I had to bring back the report card with my parents' signatures. They were on top of me all fucking weekend. Finally, on Sunday night, I gave in.

"I got all Fs— whaddya want me to say? It is what it is."

I was surprised I didn't get cracked for that answer.

"I don't like school," I told my father.

My father never liked school, either, but he wanted me to have a better life than he had. Once, he picked me up from school after I'd gotten in trouble with the nuns. On the way home in the car, he didn't say a word. This isn't so bad, I remember thinking. Then, once we got into the house and I started making my way up the stairs—pow!—he caught me in the back of my head with his boot. "You motherfucker," he said. "All the money I spend sending you to private school and this is what I get? Enough of the bullshit."

Luckily for me, the report card incident reached a more peaceful (and painless) resolution. My mother covered for me by spilling coffee on the report card to fade out the changes that I'd made. Deep down, I think my parents realized that school just wasn't for me.

Eventually, school even ruined lunch, something I'd always loved. From first to fifth grade, we could bring our own from home, but beginning in the sixth grade we had to buy our lunch from the school cafeteria. Sloppy Joes? Canned tomato soup? I wouldn't have any part of it. Instead, my mother would make me a potatoes-and-eggs sandwich or a chicken cutlet with lettuce, tomato and mayo. I'd sneak the sandwiches into my book bag. Then, at lunchtime, I went into the bathroom, locked the door, sat on the toilet, and ate my sandwiches. I prayed no one had to take a shit.

Chicken Cutlets with Broccoli Rabe

Chicken cutlets are pretty simple to do, and once you get this recipe down, you can get more creative and make about a half-dozen other dishes. Or, take the cutlet and make it into a sandwich, like my mother used to with lettuce, tomato and mayo.

>>> Go to a butcher and get a piece of chicken breast that should weigh about 3 to 4 ounces. See if you can get your butcher to cut them real thin (that's very important).

>>> For the next step you're going to need flour, eggs, bread crumbs and three clean bowls. In the first bowl put flour, in the second bowl crack four large eggs. Season the eggs with Kosher salt, crushed black pepper, Italian parsley and 2 tablespoons of Parmigiano-Reggiano cheese. Whisk the mixture together. In the third bowl put bread crumbs.

>>> Working one chicken cutlet at a time, place the chicken cutlet in the flour and cover lightly, then dip it in the egg wash and lastly in the bread crumbs. When all the cutlets are finished, let them rest in the refrigerator for an hour or so.

>>> After an hour, fill a pan a quarter full with extra-virgin olive oil and heat. When the oil is hot, fry the cutlets over medium heat. Get them nice and brown on both sides.

Broccoli Rabe (bitter greens)

>>> Saute extra-virgin olive oil and smashed garlic cloves. Brown the garlic, then add some red pepper flakes, add broccoli rabe to the pan and saute until tender. Season with Kosher salt and crushed black pepper and serve on top of the chicken cutlet. Finish with extra-virgin olive oil and top with imported sharp provolone and toasted bread crumbs.

Top: Chicken Cutlets with Broccoli Rabe.

Bottom: Macaroni cooked al dente (firm to the tooth).

I guess high school was about the time I opened my first take-out business. I'd have my mother pack me a few extra sandwiches every day, then I'd eat one and sell the others. Business was booming—that is until my friend Fat Frankie started stealing the goods. At first, I couldn't figure out what was happening to the sandwiches. Then, one day in the middle of class, I looked out the door and saw that fat bastard in the hallway dangling my lunch bag and wiping his mouth. I thought I'd solved the problem by hiding my lunch in different spots every day. Didn't matter, though—he'd always find it. They didn't call him Fat Frankie for sucking lemons.

My grades got a lot better in high school at Bishop Neumann, but not because my study habits improved. During the gas shortages of the '70s when people needed vouchers to purchase gasoline, I got them for my teachers and they all gave me passing grades. I rarely went to class. Instead, I spent my day in the audio-visual room thinking of ways to earn. I probably bumped into my teachers more at nightclubs than I did in classrooms.

But when I did attend class, I was determined to look sharp, like Uncle Raymond. Dress shirt. Tie. Shined shoes—people started calling me "Marvelous Martorano." I even began my own number and sports betting business to add to the money I made delivering dry-cleaning and painting houses. When I went into Mr. Carapucci's class, I would put the winning number on the blackboard before the bell rang. Then Carapucci would come into class and erase the number, but he was cool about it.

"Marvelous," he'd say, "that's enough." Then he'd laugh.

If there was a money making scheme, I was in the middle of it. I was determined to always have cash. It reminded me that cash was power. You couldn't buy nice things with nickels and dimes.

I even tried my hand at boxing for a while. I was going to be the next great Italian-American heavyweight. I trained at the Juniper Street Gym in South Philly under the management of Nicholas Belfiglio. They thought I had potential, so they threw me in the ring to spar with a local fighter named Matthew Franklin (In 1979, Franklin won the WBC Light Heavyweight crown, converted to Islam, and became Matthew Saad Muhammad). Belfiglio and I didn't think Franklin was going to really bang me around much, but we were wrong. After climbing out of the ring with Franklin, my headed pounded for the next three weeks. Fuck this, I thought. There's got to be a better way.

Left: Halloween party at Valentino's in Cherry Hill. We won first place. From left to right: me as Rocky Balboa, my friend Nikki as Adrian and Fat Frankie as Paulie.

Right: Young Steve starting out in the kitchen.

CHAPTER 06

Even though my father only made $166 a week at the vending company (up until the day he died), he always sent me, my mother and Nanny to the Jersey Shore for two weeks each summer no matter what. My father would come on Saturday night and leave Sunday morning to go back to work. His vacation was one week out of the year to go hunting.

He used to hunt for deer, and, if you've ever known a deer hunter, you know they can go 100 years and never come home with anything. Basically, I think that guys just want to get away from their wives and families (not that there's anything wrong with that).

When I got older, I finally came to the conclusion that there weren't any deer.

Then one time I went hunting with my father and some of the guys. I had to take a shit, and so I went deep, deep into the woods, far away from everyone else. I found a little stream and decided to set up shop there. I set down my rifle, dropped my pants to my ankles, and took a squat. Then I heard a little noise. I looked up and saw a deer. I panicked a little, grabbed the gun, and fired. I hit the thing in the hind legs, but didn't kill it and the deer had fallen into the stream. The deer made an awful sound and it broke my heart, so I put it out of its misery. Then I had to carry that motherfucker all the way back to the car. I don't think I ever went hunting again after that.

My dad, though, continued to make it a regular thing.

One weekend, I saw all these people outside of my house looking up at the window. I thought someone had died, so I rushed over to the crowd. Everyone was staring at this big buck strung up with electric wire outside the front window. My father had finally got himself a deer, and he kept that motherfucker there for what seemed like a week to show everybody that he had shot a deer—a real deer.

South Philly Style Tripe

My father, like his father, was a really great cook. He could take a scrambled egg, add anything to it, and it was delicious. When I was younger, he took me hunting and fishing in the Poconos. Ten guys rented a cabin, never took a shower and we ate like kings.

My father's favorite meal in the outdoors was tripe. He'd make it with tomato sauce, a little celery and carrots. Then he tossed in macaroni, and we ate like royalty.

>>> Get a pound of veal tripe, two cans of San Marzano tomatoes, Kosher salt, 8 tablespoons of olive oil, three cloves of garlic, a small onion, chopped Italian parsley, dry white wine, and crushed black pepper. Cut the tripe in little pieces and boil it for about an hour. Heat the olive oil and add the garlic and onions—celery and carrots, too, if you like. Saute everything until it's nice and soft. Let the garlic get golden brown. Throw the drained tripe into the pan and season it with salt and pepper. When the tripe gets a little color, hit the pan with a couple of splashes of white wine. While the liquid in the pan is reducing, put the tomatoes in a bowl and squeeze them with your hands. Add the tomatoes to the pan and season again with a little salt and pepper. Cook for about 90 minutes or until the tripe still has a little bite to it. Toss the tripe with some macaroni, freshly chopped parsley and grated Parmigiano-Reggiano cheese.

Italian Hoagie

There was a place on the board walk in Atlantic City called the Italian Village that made Italian sandwiches when I was growing up. They made a sandwich with Proscuitto and sharp provolone nothing else no oil, no tomatoes, no lettuce NOTHING. I took this sandwich to another level by adding marinated vine ripened tomatoes, fried hot peppers and extra-virgin olive oil.

>>> At your deli counter, tell them you want all your lunchmeat cut paper-thin. If the lunchmeat is not cut paper-thin, it will never be a great sandwich. Get some Prosciutto di Parma (it's the best), some slices of provolone, and some nice tomatoes. Season with Kosher salt and crushed black pepper, add a little basil and olive oil. Add a little romaine lettuce and some roasted peppers. Get a crisp Italian bread and take the insides out. Warm the bread a little in the oven. Drizzle the bread with a little olive oil. Add the prosciutto, provolone, tomatoes (onions are optional), romaine lettuce, salt, pepper, roasted peppers, a little more olive oil, basil, oregano and you're done.

When I turned 18, after graduation, hanging around with my family in Wildwood for a couple of weeks during the summer, the woods didn't cut it for me anymore. All I wanted to do was hit the beach during the day and then go out to the clubs with my friends at night. I got permission to stay through August and planned to stay with some South Philly friends who had a house for the summer. My mother took care of me like I never left the house. Each weekend she brought food, brought clean clothes and collected my dirty laundry. My father was tougher on me: He demanded that I get a job.

In high school, I had started lifting weights and was doing the boxing thing. So by that summer I was no longer the heavy-set kid they used to call "Truck" and made for a pretty imposing figure. That made me a natural to work the door as a bouncer at The Court Room night-club. I quickly gained a reputation. I didn't take shit from anybody. I didn't give a fuck who it was or who they

were with. I had a certain way of running that door, and that's the way I ran it. Respect me and the place where I worked, and I'd respect you.

Toward the end of that summer in Wildwood, I made my way up the street to another club, The Mansion, and ran into Bobby Pantano, a well-known disc jockey who worked there.

"So, what are you gonna do now?" asked Bobby.

"I don't know," I said. "What the fuck? I'm gonna go back home, I guess, and earn anyway I can."

But Bobby was aware of my passion for music and those 45s my father brought home. He had an idea.

"I'm gonna make you a DJ."

He introduced me to his manager, John Richie, a guy who was as queer as a 3-dollar bill but associated with wiseguys around the entertainment business. He offered to manage me. But first I had to buy equipment.

The cost was close to $3,000 dollars. I knew I didn't have the money and though I left for home disappointed, my mind was still at work.

Immediately, my mother knew something was wrong.

"What's the matter?" she asked.

"Nothing," I lied.

"I know something is wrong."

I told her the story, then she called my father into the kitchen.

Three-thousand dollars, I thought as my mother explained the situation to my father—that was like asking my father for a million.

"Jesus Christ. Are you kidding me?" he yelled. "That's a lot of money."

My father left the room, came back into the kitchen, and handed me the money.

"This is a loan," he said.

I bought the equipment, but knew I had to repay the loan, plus the points—just like his Atlantic City buddies.

With no money or real skills and barely an education, I went to the one place I knew I could make money. I headed for the streets, standing on the corner of 29th and Snyder, where my uncle also had a drugstore. I decided to sell produce—tomatoes, peppers, lettuce. It was a cash business—no rent, no gas, no electric.

"Insalata, insalata—three for a dollar!"

Fucking nuns, I thought. Maybe they were right, but I wasn't going to drive no truck or be on the corner for the rest of my life.

1,400 pounds, 15 reps. That's not bad for an old man...

SECTION 2

The Hits Keep Coming

CHAPTER 07

The snow-covered streets were empty outside the tiny diner in Cherry Hill, New Jersey. Inside, the scene wasn't much different, but it was warm.

"Fuck me," I thought. "Fuck this." No one in their right mind was going to come see a guy they'd never heard of play in this kind of shit. One of the biggest blizzards of 1978 and I was standing there in my sharpest suit and tie like some kind of jerk-off.

My equipment was set up on stage; two turntables, speakers, lights and five huge crates packed with 12-inch records and 45's. I had two of each song so I could mix and fade to extend a 2-minute tune into 8 minutes of magic.

I'd always had a great collection of R&B and Motown hits thanks to my father, who brought home records from work at John's Vending; however, the summer before, I was introduced to disco by a kid from the neighborhood, DJ Joey G.

One day, we were driving in my old Cadillac when he changed the station from one that played all oldies to another I'd never heard before.

"Cuz, what the fuck is this?" I asked. But it didn't matter. I was hooked as soon as I heard those symbols. I wanted to play that sound. It was the song "Ten Percent" by Double Exposure. I got my hands on all of it: "Lady, Lady, Lady" by The Boogieman Orchestra; The Temptations' Eddie Kendricks with "Date With The Rain"; and underground shit like Hocus Pocus, who supposedly cut their songs in a garage, and my favorite, "I'll Always Love My Momma" by the Intruders. (I loved that song so much that I had it tattooed on my back—the first of many.)

But that night in Cherry Hill, there was no music—just snow. Me and Frankie had lugged my equipment from South Philly all for nothing. We were supposed to work until 2 a.m., but settled with the owner and left around 11 p.m.

We packed up the equipment and drove down the street.

"Holy shit," I said. "What the fuck is that?"

A few blocks down the street from the diner, there was a line of cars a mile long. We parked, got out and walked to see what was going on. The snow was still coming down and it was a little after midnight, but there were at least two dozen people waiting to get into a new club called Valentino's. I remembered hearing about the club, but didn't think it was supposed to open for awhile. There were girls in dresses, guys in suits and big fellas speaking Italian at the door. Inside, blue and white lights danced across the crowded floor, a sea of people that led to a stage with a raised DJ booth.

"Do you fucking believe this?" said Frankie.

Hovering over turntables and a sound board stood DJ Joey G, who had spotted us and was waving Frankie and

The place of my first DJ gig.

me to the booth.

We talked for awhile, but were interrupted by a man hollering in Italian and broken English.

"You," he said, pointing to Joey G. "You gotta talk."

"What do you mean?" he said. "I'm a DJ—I don't talk."

Then the man, in his 30s and perfectly tailored from head to toe, turned and shoved a microphone in my hand and asked if I was a DJ.

"Yeah," I said.

"You, you gotta say, 'Every Monday, Tuesday and Thursday the Italiano band Calypso plays. Free buffet—all night long."

I made the announcement. From the booth, I looked down and saw the man speaking with a beautiful woman and another man. They were pointing at me and nodding, then the well-dressed man returned and introduced himself as the owner of the club.

"You a DJ? You wanna a job?"

"Sure," I said.

The next evening, as I was sitting down for a meal of Linguine Aglio e Olio with my mother and father, the phone rang. It was the secretary of the well-dressed man from Valentino's. He wanted to see me, she said.

What could he want? I hope I didn't lose the job, I thought.

I left for his office at the club in Cherry Hill and when we met, the man greeted me with open arms.

"You-a 'Long-a John's' nephew, right?" he said with a thick Italian accent. "Very nice man. Welcome. Welcome to the family."

Guiseppe "Joe" Gambino—one of three Sicilian brothers known as the "Cherry Hill Gambinos" from New York—had just hired me to work in one of the hottest nightclubs around. Everyone thought I got this job because of Uncle Raymond, but I got it own my own.

Dancing with Francine. We took 2nd place for a role in "Saturday Night Fever."

Me practicing the 'Hustle' with cousin Linda.

Linguine Aglio e Olio (garlic and oil—Sicilian Style)

This is one of my favorites—simplicity at its best. A great late night snack. All you're going to need is extra-virgin olive oil, Kosher salt, crushed red pepper, anchovies, Italian parsley and homemade toasted bread crumbs.

>>> Lets start with extra-virgin olive oil. Put some in the frying pan then add some finely chopped garlic and saute on low heat until brown. Add crushed red pepper, Kosher salt and Italian parsley.

>>> Now drop the macaroni in lightly salted boiling water. After about 3 to 4 minutes, take about 2 tablespoons of the water from the macaroni and add it to the frying pan.

>>> Now to make your toasted bread crumbs: Get some extra-virgin olive oil in the frying pan and let it get warm. Then add your store-bought or homemade bread crumbs and fry until brown. Use these bread crumbs to sprinkle on top of the dish when it's completed. You can keep these for up to 3 days.

>>> Drain the macaroni and toss with the contents from the frying pan. Top with bread crumbs. Now you've got yourself a meal!

Top: That's me on the left spinning at my friend Mickey Fatone's birthday party.

Middle: My son, Joey Martorano, when he was younger. The apple doesn't fall far from the tree.

Bottom: Joey at Cafè Martorano in Fort Lauderdale. He still spins today.

CHAPTER 08

There were only two smells in Valentino's: the food and the cologne.

Guys wore that shit by the bottle. I was no different, except I never liked people to know what I was wearing, and if they figured it out, I'd switch. Or, I'd start mixing the stuff. A little from this bottle, a little from that one. I didn't like the idea of guys in my crew using the same cologne. Plus, keeping the ladies guessing presented the opportunity for a good pick-up line.

"Steve, what are you wearing?" they'd ask. And I'd say, "It's called 'Come Follow Me.'" It worked like a charm, and being the club DJ didn't hurt none, either. There were all kinds of girls around willing to climb into the booth with me and fool around. I'd just play an extra long version of something and no one on the dance floor below had a clue.

As far as the food went, Valentino's wasn't Sunday dinner at my grandmother's, but it was pretty damn good. Joe Gambino and his brother, Sal, had a kitchen full of Italians from the Other Side working the line. During breaks or after my shift, I loved to hang out and watch the Zips cook. Zips were guys that came from It-lee. They made veal piccata, veal marsala and chicken and peppers—all good, but nothing as good as I could get at home or make myself. I always wondered why food at a restaurant didn't taste quite as good as food at home and began to see why: pre-cooked cutlets and macaroni and products like olive oil that were good, but not the best.

Rocky and me.

Picture of me pretending that's my car. Even back then I was wishing I had a Cadi-Daddy!

Veal Piccata

When I was growing up, we didn't have veal marsala in my house. We didn't have veal piccata. We didn't eat like that. But, in my house today, I make veal piccata. It's very simple.

>>> You get some really thin slices of veal. I use tenderloin. You can use the top of the round. Season the veal with Kosher salt and crushed black pepper, and heat up some extra-virgin olive oil with a little butter.

>>> When the butter starts to foam, coat the veal in all-purpose flour and put it in the frying pan. This shouldn't take more than 2 minutes. When the edges of the veal get brown, take the veal out and get rid of the oil and butter.

>>> In the same pan, add more butter, a little chicken stock, Italian parsley, juice from 1 lemon, a little Kosher salt and crushed black pepper. Then just taste it and see what else it needs. A little bit of this or a little bit of that. Now put the veal back into the pan and warm the veal up and add chopped fresh Italian parsley. Then plate and serve.

One night I blew their minds when I made a veal piccata sandwich with a double order of veal with lots of lemon flavor. "What kind of DJ cooks like this?" they asked. I said the Italian-American kind, and they cursed me in Italian. It was great.

On another occasion, Angelo Bruno and Uncle Raymond came to Valentino's for dinner. I had remembered that my Aunt Evelyn, Raymond's wife, once told me Mr. Bruno loved linguine and clams with prosciutto, so I went into the kitchen and decided to surprise him.

Mr. Bruno, a first-generation Sicilian, took a bite. Then he leaned back in his chair, touched the bridge of his thick glasses frames, and smiled.

"Who cooked this?" he asked Raymond. I stepped forward and boasted, "No cook, just a DJ." Mr. Bruno smiled.

Fresh clam stock.

Linguine with Clams and Prosciutto

This was one of Angelo Bruno's favorites. If it was good enough for the boss, it should be good enough for you, cuz. Here's how I did it for the "Docile Don":

>>> I went back into the kitchen, shucked the clams out of the shells, put in some extra-virgin olive oil, and two or three cloves of garlic and I browned them. After they got golden brown and had a nice flavor, I added a little crushed red pepper. I knew Angelo loved anchovies, so I put a little bit in there too. Then I took some slices of proscuitto and tossed it with Italian parsley then added the clams. I didn't put in any white wine because that's optional. I also salted the water for the macaroni, but I didn't drain it.

>>> When I was growing up, my mother used to take the macaroni right out of the pot when the water was boiling and the macaroni was cooking.

>>> I took tongs and lifted the macaroni out the pot while the pot was still boiling, let the water drain off, tossed it in with the clam sauce, and sent it out to Mr. Bruno. He loved it. You will, too. And, please, no grated cheese.

>>> That's the old-school way. For the classic version, use a smaller clam, like a littleneck, but keep it in the shell and add some Italian parsley. Skip the prosciutto and anchovies, and use a dry white wine to steam the clams open.

I knew how to cook by helping my mother and grandmother in the kitchen. South Philly-style cooking is really just peasant-style cooking. You make due with what you have. We were poor when I was young, so when I was hungry and there wasn't anything in the house to eat I'd make a mayo sandwich, which was just sliced bread, lettuce, tomato and a little mayo—I didn't need any fucking meat. When I was a little older and my kitchen skills improved, I started experimenting with eggs. Then I'd get brave, adding mushrooms, peppers, onions and maybe some potatoes. That's how I started cooking—watching and learning, then trying it on my own. Never in a million years did I think I'd go from mayo sandwiches to cooking linguine and clams with prosciutto for Angelo Bruno, the most powerful man in Philadelphia. And even though I continued to concentrate on my music, that experience with Mr. Bruno encouraged me to make more.

My mother and me in my kitchen in South Florida.

CHAPTER 09

About a year after I'd been hired by the Gambinos, I hooked up with a girl bartender of theirs. After shutting down the club one night, we went to a diner across the street for something to eat and, later, got a room where I knocked her goofy. Early the next morning, I drove the girl back to her car. Almost immediately, we were surrounded by three other cars.

It's a hit, I thought.

"Oh, shit," she said. "It's John."

"Who the fuck is John?"

Then a guy got out of one of the cars, opened up my passenger door and made the girl get out, and gave me a warning.

"Stay the fuck away from my girl or you'll get your legs broke."

I didn't know how many other guys were in the cars or if this guy had a gun, so I played it safe, said fuck this, and took off.

When I got home, I was concerned about what had happened and prepared for the worst. I called my friend Mikey Coppola and told him the story.

"Listen," I told Mikey. "we gotta be ready for these guys tonight if they show up again. I'll be holding. Make sure you've got something, too."

My father called me downstairs. He had been at home recovering from a work accident (a 1,200-pound fence fell on him while he was making deliveries) in which he broke his legs and was laid up in a body cast and confined to bed. He was resting in the parlor and heard every word of the conversation on the extension.

"Son, what do you need a fucking gun for?" he said.

I told him the story and asked him not to say anything to Uncle Raymond. He was furious. I didn't want to get him upset because of his condition, but what could I do? He was my father. He told me he would take care of it. Still, I left for work with my piece.

I wasn't at the club long before Angelo Bruno walked through the door with Sonny Riccobene and my uncle.

"Where's Joe Gambino?" Angelo demanded. "Where's Sal?"

The men sat in the back of the restaurant and talked about what had happened with me and the girl. Fifteen minutes later, Joe Gambino arrived and went over to their table.

Joe knew the girl's boyfriend, John. He knew where he was at.

The next day, Uncle Raymond sent two of his men to the boyfriend's house. They knocked on the door and his wife answered. She tried to bluff and acted like he wasn't at home, but it didn't take long for Raymond's men to find him. They held a gun to his head, dragged him out of the house, and shoved him into the backseat of a car. When they got to John's Vending, they dragged the guy into Raymond's office. Then the boyfriend crawled to where Raymond was sitting.

"Jesus!" he cried. "Please—don't kill me. I'm in love with her. God—don't kill me. I saw her with your nephew and I was jealous. I'm sorry. I'm sorry. I'll leave. I'll leave her, leave the country—whatever you want. Just don't kill me."

"Be careful who you threaten like that," Raymond said.

And just like that, they let the boyfriend go. I always wondered why they let him go, but eventually I realized Uncle Raymond didn't need to raise his hand to be feared.

About a week later, I ran into my uncle and he told me what had happened.

"You have more courage in your pinky nail than that guy had in his whole body," said my uncle. "But watch yourself. You never know when some punk wants to make a name for himself."

CHAPTER 10

When the cops and paramedics hovered over Philip Testa's body in front of the Philadelphia boss' bombed out Girard Estates home, the crowd that had gathered turned angry. The way those motherfucking cops had treated Mr. Bruno was still fresh in their minds.

It was hard to forget that just a year earlier, in 1980, Bruno was the one dead by assassination—in the car, eyes closed and mouth open like a gutted trophy deer on the front lawn of a hunter. It was disrespectful the way the cops just left him like that for everyone to see.

When I found out about Mr. Bruno, I was spinning records at the London Victory Club in Center City. Around 7 p.m. on that fateful night I took a break and hurried past the coat room. On the way, I stopped to watch breaking news on the TV—Angelo Bruno had been assassinated. The Docile Don was being dropped off at his home by John Stanfa, a soldier. Gunmen opened up on Angelo, killing him and wounding Stanfa. It was considered one of the biggest gangland slayings in mob history. It was too bad; Mr. Bruno was such a gentleman. Once, he even asked for my advice about the nightclub business. I was honored.

For days and weeks after the assassination, Bruno's image was everywhere in Philadelphia—on the news and in the papers. Speculation followed: Who was going to be Philly's new boss? The media pegged four men—Testa, Frank Sindone, Chickie Narducci, and Raymond "Long John" Martorano—as Bruno's likely successors.

The pick was Philip Testa, a close family friend and father to my friend Salvie. Testa was called "The Chicken Man." He had a pock-marked face and a beak of a nose, but no one ever called Testa "The Chicken Man" to his face; that was a media thing. Among the people I knew in South Philly, he was respected and, everyone had assumed, well liked.

When you can't make your own, Tony Luke's in South Philly is one of the bests!

Mussels Marinara

After Phil Testa was killed, shit hit the fan.

One night I was at Anton's, a bar owned by my uncle, when my father answered the phone and his face drained.

"Jesus Christ," my father said. "They killed 'Chickie.'"

"Chickie" was Frank Narducci, one of the capos who allegedly plotted the bombing that killed mob boss Phil Testa, "The Chicken Man." Narducci was shot 10 times in January 1982, less than a year after the Testa hit. It was rumored that the New York Commission ordered Narducci hit because the murder of Testa had not been sanctioned.

I'll never forget that night because my dad and I were eating mussels marinara when the call came. And I knew that Chickie loved my Mussels Marinara.

>>> Back in the day the only way to clean mussels the right way was to put them in the washing machine. So we used to buy old school washing machines and put the mussels in like we were washing clothes. Today we have great mussels, PEI (prince edward mussels), that don't require that kind of cleaning.

>>> Heat some extra-virgin olive oil, brown some fresh garlic, add imported San Marzano tomatoes and season with Kosher salt and crushed black pepper. Cook for about 10 minutes then throw your mussels in with some fresh basil. Cook until they open. Discard any mussels that don't open.

But after Bruno was assassinated in a hit that didn't appear to have the blessing of The New York Commission, things got messy.

In October, Frank Sindone, a guy with big glasses and a small mouth, was found with three bullets in his head behind a South Philly store. It was payback, they said, for his alleged role in Bruno's death.

Now it was Testa's turn. The crowd that had gathered in Girard Estates got ugly as the cops sorted through the evidence and the hot metal from the bomb packed with nails that had ripped through "The Chicken Man" and his home.

"Leave him alone," they screamed.

I found a pay phone and put in a call to make sure Uncle Raymond was OK. Then we went to Fat Frankie's house and sat on the front step.

"What the fuck is going on in Philly?" said Fat Frankie, who finally unwrapped the cheesesteak he had been carrying since we arrived.

I wondered the same thing.

CHAPTER 11

Around the same time as the Phil Testa incident, Fat Frankie and me got our hands on about 1,000 pills from my cousin as a way to make a little extra money. In 1982, pills were simply part of the culture, and Frankie and me felt comfortable with my cousin. We were just looking for a way to earn a few extra bucks.

The plan was pretty simple: my cousin was going to front the pills, take 30 percent, and then we'd split the rest. Me and Frankie hooked up with a Zip named Joe to deal half of the stuff. But after only 24 hours, Joe the Italian had disappeared, along with the pills and any chance of making back our money.

"It'll be alright," said Frankie. "He's your cousin. He'll understand."

To make up for the loss, we brought our half of the pills to the London Victory Club in Center City. While working that night, I gave them to a guy I knew from my neighborhood, Mike. I walked out of the club and saw people running in the middle of the street. I walked over and saw Mikey. He was on his hands and knees and all fucked up. He had dropped the bag of pills in the street and people were diving for them. I saw that there were cops all over the place and I left.

The next morning, I went looking for Mikey but he didn't have any money. I thought about smacking him, but where would that get me? I decided to deal with him later. Then I went to my cousin and told him the story.

"What the fuck do you want me to do?" said my cousin.

"Cuz, you're my fucking cousin. Come on, cuz, help me out here."

"Help you out, cuz? It's business." He shrugged. "It's got nothing to do with us being cousins."

He was my cousin. I loved him and knew it was just business.

Clams Pavarotti

My cousin Georgie and I used to go to The Saloon every Monday night. Georgie changed his shoes four times a day back then and always wore sharp clothes. We'd swallow down a couple of 714s (Quaaludes) with a bottle of wine, and eat the same thing every time: Clams Pavarotti, Saloon Salad, homemade ravioli and Lobster Franchese with jumbo lump crab meat. And Saloon desserts? Fuhgeddaboudit!

At Café Martorano, we call this dish Stuffed Clams.

>>> Steam a dozen Quahog clams. Remove the clams, and keep the shells and juice. Dice four celery stalks, one large yellow onion and six cloves of garlic. Saute the celery, onions and garlic. When the vegetables start to sweat, add a dozen U-10 shrimp, cleaned and cut into pieces. Saute until the shrimp become translucent (it takes about a minute). Add a little flour until the mixture is thick then add 1/4 cup heavy cream and stir. Chop the clams that have been saved. In a separate bowl, combine the clams, a pound of jumbo lump crab meat, four sprigs of thyme (chopped) and the reserved clam juice. Stuff the clam shells with the mixture and top with the Béchamel sauce. Sprinkle with Parmigiano-Reggiano cheese and bake until the Béchamel is golden brown.

CHAPTER 12

Moving pills wasn't my thing, but I was still a great fucking DJ, so I decided to stick with what I knew. I started spinning at HB's, a night club in Northeast Philly, on Wednesday nights. Great decision. The girls were gorgeous.

One night, up in the DJ booth, Mikey Coppola and me looked over the dance floor. Another night, another chance to get laid.

"What about that girl?" asked Mikey.

"Been there. Done that, cuz."

Even before my career had taken off, girls came without much effort. Everyone wanted to be with the DJ; it was an unwritten rule. But by the time I had landed at HB's, I was a known guy: Steve "Marvelous" Martorano. And if my name didn't ring a bell, my Uncle Raymond's surely did. Ever since shit started going haywire in Philly, seeing his name and photo in the newspapers and on TV was a fairly regular thing.

Out of the corner of my eye, I saw a pretty girl leaning back with her foot propped against the wall. She wasn't talking or dancing.

"There," I said. I grabbed Mikey. "I'm going to marry that one. Right there."

He knew I was full of shit.

"Yeah, and you're going to marry that one … and that one … and that one, too."

He was right, but I ignored him and left to introduce myself.

"I'm Steve Martorano," I said, figuring she'd heard of the Martoranos.

The name didn't immediately register, but she said hi, and told me her name was Debbie.

Then I grabbed her hand and we headed for the dance floor. (By the way, I am a great dancer. Me and my friend Francine took second place in a hustle contest to be in the movie "Saturday Night Fever.")

"Don't you know who I am?"

She didn't.

"You've never heard of me? Steve Martorano?"

"You're the DJ," she said. "I love your music."

"I would like to take you to dinner Sunday night and bounce around South Philly."

She agreed, but when the time came to take her out, I was too busy on the street. I canceled once, twice, three times. By then, she was mad at me. In my defense, the drive to Northeast Philadelphia was only about 20 minutes, but the place was like a foreign country to a South Philly guy like me. So the next time I saw her at the club, I gave her my pinky ring and told her, "Now I have to keep our date to get my ring back."

She still didn't believe me. But I kept my promise and came back for my ring. Four months later, I gave her another ring—and that one was to keep.

Sammie, Dino and Frankie.
My Rat Pack.

Yo Cuz

SECTION 3

From the Basement Up

My mother's house.

CHAPTER 13

Guys like One-Eyed Charlie came to Anton's for only two things: booze and gambling.

Anton's was a South Philly joint on the corner of 11th and Ellsworth. It had a sign out front, a kitchen in the tiny basement and a second floor for parties that was used more often for storage and talking family business. As far as the city was concerned, the bar belonged to my father. In reality, it was Uncle Raymond's place.

Charlie was a regular who wore a patch over his right eye, and no one seemed to know how he lost it or whether he was just fucking around. Charlie was a bookmaker. He made a living off dollars, quarters and dimes, getting his cut from off-track bets made on the spot. But he was a dying breed—like the bar itself.

When the casinos first opened in Atlantic City, people were running down to the shore as fast as they could print money. Places like Anton's were hurting for business, so anything that could help a neighborhood place pay the electric or the gas or the rent was a beautiful fucking thing. Illegal poker machines seemed like a gift from God, but even that wasn't enough.

Old-timers formed a line at the door before we opened in the morning and usually stayed until 4 or 5 p.m., doing their daily bullshit like taking numbers and borrowing money. They sat on the stools and played cards between rounds of Cutty Sark and Rolling Rock. My father, who had never quite recovered from his work accident, limped from customer to customer as they called out:

"Joe, give us a shot, beer and a roast pork sandwich without provolone."

Shot? Beer? Quarters? It was never going to add up for my poor father. He could save all the nickels and dimes he wanted, but I knew you had to spend money to make it. So how could I make it?

A family get together. Even then I was in the kitchen—I'm the only one with an apron on. Left to right: Me, Cuz John, Cuz Raymond, Aunt Philli, Grand Pop, Little Raymond, Aunt Evelyn, My Father and Uncle John.

Roast Pork Sandwiches

Salvie Testa was a close dear friend of mine who was killed a couple years after his dad was hit. His dad was "The Chicken Man" who was blown up with a nail bomb. Rumored to have been involved in 15 hits, Salvie was a capo under mob boss Nicky Scarfo and considered a very violent individual, although I seldom saw that side of him.

I'm not sure who ordered the murder of Salvie Testa in September 1984, but it was believed to be Scarfo. A paranoid person, Scarfo either imagined or believed that Salvie couldn't be trusted.

Before he died, Salvie used to come to Anton's and loved my roast pork sandwiches. When I make them today, I think of him.

>>> Take a pork butt, season it with Kosher salt and crushed black pepper, garlic powder, garlic cloves and put it in a roasting pan. Add a little water, hot cherry peppers, hot cherry pepper juice and a bay leaf to the pan and cover it with foil. Place it in the oven at 350 degrees, then cook it for 2 to 2½ hours. When it's done, put it in the refrigerator overnight to make it nice and cold.

>>> The next day, slice the pork while it's cold, add it back to the juices, and heat it all up. One of the keys to this sandwich is having great bread and excellent provolone, not that pre-sliced shit you find in a fucking deli today.

Top: At Anton's. As you can see that was the first TV that played movies in a restaurant under my command. The first movie was "The Godfather."

Middle: Michael Cappola and me in the late '70s.

Bottom: Anton's on 11th street.

CHAPTER 14

On most mornings before Anton's opened, I put in credits in the poker machines without paying and played until I hit. Stupid move, but I needed some money. I'd pay myself ($500 here and there), put the money aside, and later go out and buy things for the bar—mostly pots, pans and quality Italian food products. I never spent the money on myself. It wasn't long before my father figured out the scam, but by that time I'd gotten what I needed for the restaurant.

Then I started thinking big.

One of my cousins, Ronnie Durante, had recently opened Philadelphia's first video store, South Philly Video on 11th and Oregon. I took my poker winnings and bought one of Ronnie's big-ass video machines and picked up a few movies. I was going to put on a "Godfather" night at the bar. Playing a movie in a restaurant or bar had never been done before as far as I knew. I was just trying to be original. People loved food. They loved "The Godfather." Why not combine the two? And with a great jukebox? It was a no-brainer.

I explained the idea to my father—we'd hold an all-you-can-eat Spaghetti and Crabs night and offer entertainment for $9.95, just like Atlantic City. I showed him the VCR.

"Look at this," I said, "a video machine."

"What's this? A what? Video machine?"

"Movies," I said. "It plays videos—movies, Da'. We're gonna have a 'Godfather' night on Monday."

"Son," he said, "people come here to drink and have fun. No one wants to watch a fucking movie."

"Da', listen, it's gonna work."

Spaghetti and Crabs

Fucking nobody makes this anymore, and I don't know why. It's incredible. The first time I did a dish like this at Anton's, people lined up around the block to get a taste.

>>> The thing to remember here is that this isn't a crab sauce, but a crab gravy. Take three cans of San Marzanos tomatoes and crush them in a bowl with your hands. Get about 25 hard-shell crabs—good ones, like Maryland blue crabs—and make sure you or the fishmonger clean them. Add some olive oil and a few cloves of garlic in a pan, then cook the crabs until they get nice and red. Then add some Kosher salt, crushed black pepper, garlic powder and a little crushed red pepper. Add the tomatoes and some fresh basil. Cover the pot and simmer for an hour and 40 minutes, and it's done. I think this gravy is best with spaghetti. But you can use any cut of macaroni you want, cuz—it's your dinner table. It's a great summer meal.

PLEASE no grated cheese on this dish. My Grandmother would roll over in her grave. May she rest in peace.

Over the next few days, I made fliers and put them up around the bar. Then I turned my attention to cleaning the bar, making it look and smell like a place where you'd actually like to eat. A few hours before the big night, I got out a bottle of furniture polish and some Pine-Sol, just like my mother used to do when she cleaned the steps in front of our house.

"What are you, some kind of sissy?' teased the old-timers. If they weren't old-timers, I would've stuffed the polish can up their asses.

Five o'clock rolled around and the guys headed home, but outside a line to get into Anton's began to snake around the corner. Before we re-opened for dinner, I went to the basement to help Carmela, a neighborhood lady, who was the restaurant cook. Then I returned to the bar and began seating customers. I popped in the movie and served dinner. No one said a word.

When the film ended, the crowd stood up and clapped. As the people cheered, my father pulled me aside and whispered.

"What are we showing next week, son?"

Steve's Father, second to left, at 19 years old and his crew.

CHAPTER 15

A week after "The Godfather" night success, my father was ready to do it again, but I tried to explain that it was something you couldn't do every day.

He didn't listen and planned an all-you-can-eat spaghetti night for $5.95. It was nothing special and it flopped as I had predicted. Worse, he was pissed off I was right. Then I told him about another idea.

"Let's do a clam bar," I said. "There's nothing like that around here—you gotta go to Atlantic City for that kind of shit."

"What's this going to cost me?" he asked.

He reluctantly agreed, but before we could pull something like that off in Anton's, we needed to buy a clam sink. I made a call to a friend of mine and had him make something small for us.

A few days later, the phone rang. It was my father.

"Get your ass to the bar," he said. "Wait 'til you see your fucking piece of art."

I went to the bar and headed for the basement. My father hovered over the new sink. He was furious.

"What do you want me to say? It's a clam sink, Da'."

"One-thousand dollars," he said.

"It's a sink, Da'. Hook it up. We need it to clean the clams."

"One-thousand fucking dollars."

A few days later, on Saturday morning, my father was still pissed. I ignored him, started cleaning the clams, and by the afternoon Carmela and I began to cook. That night I had to spin records at a club called Cachet on Broad Street, so I tried to get everything lined up before I left.

When I returned home from spinning around 5 a.m., my father was still up.

"We sold out of clams," he said. "They were eating clams like they were for free. We need more for tomorrow."

Fuck this, I thought. Not even a "thank you" or "good idea," just "make it work." I didn't need to deal with that kind of bullshit. One day he was hot, and the next day cold. My father would never understand you needed to spend money to make it, plain and simple. I was tired of trying to turn his bar into something it wasn't. He was my father, I loved him, and I knew he was just trying to do what was right. But his way was not my way.

I'd always worked on my own. My first job was shining shoes with my cousin Ronnie outside Horn and Hardart's (an upscale diner), and inside neighborhood bars, then we'd walk the streets and sell soft pretzels. Even when I was in business with the Gambinos, I was really my own boss. That's how I worked best.

It was time, I decided, to open a place of my own.

Poster signed by Sylvester Stallone to me in Café Martorano.

His whole life was a million-to-one shot.
ROCKY
Champion of Good TASTE!
ROBERT CHARTOFF - IRWIN WINKLER PRODUCTION · A JOHN G. AVILDSEN FILM · STARRING SYLVESTER STALLONE IN "ROCKY"
ALSO STARRING TALIA SHIRE · BURT YOUNG · CARL WEATHERS · AND BURGESS MEREDITH AS MICKEY · WRITTEN BY SYLVESTER STALLONE
PRODUCED BY IRWIN WINKLER AND ROBERT CHARTOFF · DIRECTED BY JOHN G. AVILDSEN · EXECUTIVE PRODUCER GENE KIRKWOOD · MUSIC BY BILL CONTI
PG PARENTAL GUIDANCE SUGGESTED
ORIGINAL MOTION PICTURE SOUNDTRACK ALBUM AND TAPE AVAILABLE ON UNITED ARTISTS RECORDS
United Artists
A Transamerica Company

CHAPTER 16

My new business, Steve's Italian Kitchen, wasn't really much of a kitchen at all. Inside my one-bedroom apartment, I put a meat slicer on the counter in the kitchen, fresh cold-cuts in the refrigerator, and I was in business. Outside, on the street, there was no room for parking, and I often left my car running and double-parked while I unloaded the groceries for making sandwiches.

During the mornings, I'd make fliers by hand: "Steve's Italian Kitchen—The Best Hoagies in Philly." For the next three hours, I'd go to different neighborhoods, passing them out to people on the street and putting them on cars and in mailboxes. Then I'd go home and wait for the phone to ring. It never did, and I'd leave for the night to spin records, disappointed. But I fought through the discouragement and did it all again the next day.

With my father's blessing, I even began listing Anton's address on the fliers in hopes of legitimizing what I was doing. But after a month of hard work, I was still throwing good food in the trash and flushing money down the toilet—but I believed in myself. No one could have told me any different.

Three months into my venture, the phone finally rang. It was 8 p.m. and I was just about to call it quits for the day and go out to work at the clubs.

"I want two Italian hoagies," said the lady on the other end of the line.

I sliced the lunch meat and tomatoes, chopped the lettuce and onions, made the hoagies and then delivered them. The bill came to $7.80 and the lady gave me a $2.20 tip. My first sale. I was busting with pride. This was it, I thought, my big break—on my own. What a feeling. It was like getting a girl's number.

The next morning I got up early to prepare for the day ahead. The phone, I figured, would be ringing off the hook. I went out into the street, handed out my fliers, and hustled home to take the orders. Plus, I wanted to be home when my first customer called to tell me how great those sandwiches were.

The phone didn't ring.

It got late, and, again, I wrapped up the lunch meat, cleaned the slicer, and got ready for the club. At 8 p.m., the phone rang. It was my first customer—Mrs. Right, I called her, because she knew I made the right hoagie for her.

"I want two more hoagies," said the lady. "Those first two were delicious."

It was a small step, but I wasn't going to look back. Repeat business—that's was going to be the start of my success.

CHAPTER 17

By the end of that first year in 1983, my sandwich business had picked up considerably.

Family and friends were a big help, especially Debbie. We were getting married in a few months and even though she had a job at a bank, I wanted to make sure I was able to provide for my family.

I was going non-stop. Sandwich guy by day, DJ by night and then a pain began to develop in my chest. But I figured it would go away once business got better. With all the running in and out of the apartment, I hardly noticed anything was wrong. No one noticed anything at all, except my landlord.

"You got a business going on in there?" he asked. "I'm calling the cops."

"Business?" I said. "I ain't got no business. I'm a DJ, cuz."

"That's not what I heard," he said. "Tell it to the cops."

"Tell it to your mother," I said.

Fuck. I called Fat Frankie and told him to bring his truck. When he arrived, we grabbed the fliers and loaded the slicer and fridge inside. Then we headed for my mother's basement on Newkirk Street.

It ended up being one of my best business moves. I didn't have to pay for rent, gas, electric or a phone. My mom was always around to answer the phone to take orders and helped wash pots and pans. We added spaghetti and meatballs, chicken cutlet and broccoli rabe sandwiches, veal parm sandwiches, homemade soups and spaghetti with crabs on Friday.

First advertisement in the local paper.

Veal Parm Sandwich

Another great sandwich that's best on crusty Italian bread or a roll. I like mine with fried Italian long hot peppers.

>>> Use the same breading procedure as you do with the chicken cutlets (Page 45), and saute the veal cutlet until it's golden brown. Remove from the pan and top with some Sunday Gravy (or one of my own famous jarred sauces). Top with fresh mozzarella and fresh basil. Melt under a broiler or place in a hot oven. Serve on some of that great Italian bread.

After having stayed up all night spinning records, I'd get up early in the morning and prepare the day's food, and when I was done, I'd plop on the couch in Mom's parlor.

"Oh, look at my son, my poor baby. He's tired. Rest, rest, rest."

And she was right, I was tired. Things had never been busier, my business never better. I still didn't feel 100 percent, so I decided to go to my doctor, Vincent Baldino.

Left: My mother and father's wedding.

Right: My mother outside her house on Newkirk Street.

CHAPTER 18

I looked at myself in the mirror of the doctor's office. My face was thin, my clothes didn't fit and dark circles had formed around my eyes. For the last year, I had been like a shark, always on the move. I was scared shitless to sleep: The Martoranos had a history of closing their eyes and never waking up from heart problems.

Added to the pressure of working two jobs and trying to keep a new business afloat, my family was being torn apart. In 1983, my cousin Georgie Martorano was convicted and sentenced to life without parole for running a $75 million-a-year drug ring. (I think it was a bullshit charge. He was convicted, fine. But he's been in for 27 years, becoming the longest-serving non-violent offender in U.S. history. Bullshit charge or not, he's done his time. He needs to come home.) A few months later in 1984, things went from bad to worse when Uncle Raymond was tried, convicted and sentenced to life in prison for the murder of a union boss, John McCullough.

The doctor finished his tests. He'd have the results in a few days. I left the office, went to a neighborhood church, and knelt in front of a statue of the Blessed Mother.

"Don't let me die," I prayed. "Not yet, I have so much more to do." I made a deal with the Blessed Mother. If my tests come back normal, I'd pray to her forever. Imagine that—trying to make a deal with the Blessed Mother.

Despite my run-ins with the nuns at King of Peace, I had always been a fairly religious child. Once, when I was 7 or 8, I even had a dream: An airplane landed in the alley behind our row house, then the pope came out from the plane and called to me, "Come with me, son." After that, I made a small altar in my bedroom and, at times, considered becoming a priest. But my family didn't encourage things like that. Religion—turning the other cheek—was a weakness.

I felt as conflicted then as I did now praying in the church. I promised myself to give up the drinking and partying.

I went home and drew a dove—the symbol of the Holy Spirit—on my fliers. I was going to change my life and pray—morning, noon and night. But even in prayer, I was a hustler. Every time I needed something, I'd get on my knees and pray and try to make a deal.

A statue given to me by my friend, Danny, of the "Blessed Mother and Baby Jesus."

CHAPTER 19

Thanks to good news from the doctor, I was finally able to sleep. It was anxiety, he said—not my heart.

I kept my promises to God. (Mostly.) For the first time in my life, I began reading the Bible, and on the weekends I went on religious retreats. At the same time, I was pulling back from my work in the clubs, which pleased Debbie.

Everything seemed to be going well. Then, two weeks before our wedding, I awoke to screaming.

"He's dead, he's dead. My husband is dead," cried my mother.

Two weeks before I got married, my father was at Torano's. Torano's is a famous South Philly restaurant formerly known as Cuz's Little Italy and owned by Uncle Raymond. That night, my father locked up, paid everyone, and went home. He had to have been feeling pretty good because when he got home he apparently had gone into the freezer for some scrapple for the next morning's breakfast and bull's balls for a Palm Sunday dinner delicacy, and left the meat on the counter to defrost. Then it looked like he had laid down to watch TV. He fell asleep, and never woke up. It was a massive heart attack. He was only 54.

My mother and Nanny went into the kitchen with Debbie. They cried and screamed. I was left alone in the parlor with the body of my father. I called my uncles, then the undertaker. I sat and waited by myself, staring at the body of my father. There were a lot of things I said I shouldn't have. So I leaned over, kissed him, told him I was sorry and that I loved him.

George Martorano kissing Great Grandson Joey, aka 'Buges,' Martorano.

When the undertaker arrived, I helped put my father in a bag and I zipped it shut. Because my father was so large, I had to help carry him to the hearse. I gave the undertaker some money and left to buy my father a suit. I decided that Joe Martorano was finally going to get something new and I was paying for it.

The authorities released Uncle Raymond for the memorial service. Before he arrived, cops were posted on the corners in front of the funeral home. Television crews set up on the street and one of their helicopters hovered in the air above. Raymond arrived at the door. His feet and hands were shackled and he was escorted by two officers. I got fucking mad and started motherfucking them, their mothers, and their fathers.

"I'm not going to embarrass my nephew and his family like this," said Uncle Raymond before entering the funeral home. "Take me back."

A week after we buried my father, Uncle John, one of my father's brothers, called me into his office. He wanted to talk.

"Talk about what," I said

It's time to come with us.

"What? Loading trucks? Fixing jukeboxes? No, no, no—forget about that."

"You gotta do the right thing," he said. "You gotta take up for your father. It's time to come with us."

All I could think of was the $166 a week my father made. I wasn't going to end up like my father; my uncle's offer was unacceptable. I had a lot of anger in me. So, I swallowed hard and prayed to the Blessed Mother.

"I got God in my life. That's not the way he wants me to go."

He stared at me like I had three fucking heads. It's amazing. If he would've gotten sick, the first thing he would have done is drop to his knees and start praying.

"OK, kid. Do what you gotta do. But remember: One day you'll be with us."

"Kiss my ass," I said under my breath.

I found a pay phone and called Debbie.

"You know what he asked me, don't you?" I said.

"Yeah," she said. "I kinda figured."

"I told him that life was over for me," I said.

Left: Steve's Mother and Father out on Saturday Night. Their only night of the week out.

Right: Steve's Nanny, Sue Durante; Steve's mother's, mother, on the boardwalk in Atlantic City. Gorgeous!

CHAPTER 20

In the days leading up to our wedding, my mother began sorting through my father's belongings. She handed me a worn piece of tiny paper that had been carefully folded and refolded. On the paper were a lot of numbers and initials written in what looked to be code of men who owed my father money. Guys like my father never had a bank account. All he owned was either in his pocket or on the street.

We spent all of my father's insurance money on the funeral. It was my responsibility to go and collect the money that was owed to my family. Thousands of dollars on the street were due. My father always taught me that you didn't want the guy to pay his loan off—you wanted the juice on the loan. No more loan, no more juice coming. On the street, the custom was that if the loan shark lent you money then died, the debt was squashed. But we needed the money. That tradition wasn't going to work for me.

Motherfucker, I thought. Maybe this was the last thing I'd have to do before starting over. This had to be some kind of test. I hoped people would do the right thing and I could move on.

One by one, I tracked down the men over the course of the next few days.

"Oh, I just paid him last month," said one guy.

"Your dad said we were even, kid," said another.

"He said I didn't own him the whole thing," said a third asshole.

Fuck this, I thought. That turning the other cheek shit didn't work here on the street.

I found one man in a bar and he gave me the same story as the others, but by now I was angry and lost control. I threw the motherfucker against the wall and put my hands around his neck. His eyes bulged and he rifled through his pockets for his wallet.

"Just take it," he said. "Take it all."

It wasn't even half of what he owed, but I crumpled the bills, put them in my pocket, and spit in his face.

"That's my father's money, you motherfucker," I said. "Now it's mine. Pay me the rest tomorrow or I'll finish what I started."

CHAPTER 21

Unfortunately for me and Debbie, my father's death was just one tragedy in our streak of bad luck.

A year or so before we met at HB's, her mother died from cancer. While we were dating, her father—a real sweetheart of a guy who loved to gamble—passed on too. Then, a few months before we got married, her brother Jimmy died in a house fire. Jimmy had been at Debbie's apartment the night of the accident, a Sunday dinner and a movie, escape from New York.

"Why don't you sleep on the couch instead of driving home?" I asked Jimmy.

"No, no, I want to go home and sleep in my own bed," he said.

Around 3 or 4 in the morning, the phone rang. It was Debbie's cousin Phillip. He lived across the street from Jimmy and called to say there was a fire at Debbie's brother's house. We found out later that Jimmy was dozing on the couch with a cigarette in his hand, and ashes must have fallen into the couch before he went to bed. When we got to the house the neighbors said there were no flames, just a lot of smoke. They said Jimmy was screaming for help through an open window and the house was engulfed in smoke. He tried to get out, but was overcome and died.

Fusilli Pollo

Dishes like this one remind me of hanging out with Jimmy in Debbie's apartment, eating and watching movies. Jimmy was a great kid, like the brother I never had.

>>> Start with an 8-ounce piece of chicken cutlet that has already been cooked. Heat up some extra-virgin olive oil and brown some fresh garlic. Then throw in some hot and sweet peppers and saute until soft. Toss in the cooked chicken and a little white wine, imported San Marzano tomatoes, Kosher salt, crushed black pepper, Parmigiano-Reggiano cheese and fresh basil. Cook until done. (Pictured Left)

Debbie's Brother, Jimmy Marrone (left) with his best friend, Dennis Meyer.

Fried Mozzarella

This is a family favorite and very easy to prepare. We make our own mozzarella. You can see the steps to making fresh homemade mozzarella on the right. You must use home-made cows' milk mozzarella bought from your local deli for this dish.

>>> Take about a half inch of fresh mozzarella and bread the pieces by following my standard breading procedure (flour, seasoned egg wash and seasoned bread crumbs). In a shallow deep pan, heat up some extra-virgin olive oil. Fry the pieces until golden brown and then place in another pan and put into the oven at 350 degrees until soft.

>>> At our restaurants, we serve these with either a white or red sauce.

> For the white, saute some garlic in extra-virgin olive oil until the garlic gets brown. Add one or two anchovies, Italian parsley and a little chicken stock. When the anchovies have melted, take the pan off the heat and add some lightly salted butter and move around until completely melted. Remove the mozzarella from the oven and top with sauce.

> For the red, top with your favorite marinara sauce, or if you're really lucky you'll be able to use my own famous jarred sauces.

And then, two weeks before we got married, my father died suddenly. It was like a black cloud over our heads.

I was mad for a long time. I couldn't sleep, that's for damn sure. Every time I went to sleep, I heard my mother screaming. I'd wake up in a sweat and run downstairs, but it was just a nightmare. I had a lot of anger in me because my father was never going to see me succeed or reap the benefits of that success. If that wasn't bad enough, the black cloud didn't end with my father's death. A few years afterward, Debbie got pregnant. We didn't have much money, but were happy and excited. Everyone was looking forward to a new life in the family after so much death. Things mostly went OK, but her due date came and went and nothing happened. Three weeks past the due date, we decided to help things along.

There was this old wives' tale in South Philly that if your wife was late, you drove her up and down Delaware Avenue and over the railroad tracks there. Supposedly, going over the tracks would make women go into labor. We gave it a shot. Nothing happened at first, and then—bang!—Debbie's water broke and I drove her to the hospital.

I waited in the lobby thinking that we were going to have a regular delivery, but by the time I had filled out the paperwork, doctors and nurses were running everywhere.

"What's going on?" I asked.

"We had an emergency C-section for your wife," said a nurse. "The baby inhaled part of the meconium and it's blocking his airway."

What the fuck? Debbie's mother, father and brother die, my father's gone, and now this? If my son dies, I swear I'm gonna kill this fucking doctor, I thought. The nurse led me to a waiting room. I sat alone and cried like a baby. I bowed my head and prayed for God to save my son.

But then I heard a baby cry. Loud, like a motherfucker. The nurse wheeled the baby to me and said, "Mr. Martorano, you're the proud father of a baby boy."

The baby was alive, thank God, but they put him in an incubator and he would need to use a respirator to breathe. But the main thing was that he was alive and would eventually be OK—that's all that mattered.

I put my finger through a hole in the incubator. My hand touched the baby's hand, and I was the first to touch my son. (Even today my son, now 23, knows the story and knows that his dad was the first to touch his hand.)

We named the baby Joey in honor of my father, and the black cloud that was following us seemed to finally disappear.

CHAPTER 22

Shortly after Debbie and I were married—just a few months after my father had passed—we moved into a townhouse in Northeast Philadelphia. Given all that had recently happened, it was probably best to leave the neighborhood for awhile and make a clean start. But, unlike South Philly, this neighborhood had a large Jewish population and wasn't known for its Italian food. However, there were a number of restaurants in the area, and though none of them were worth a shit, they appeared to have a good but mostly older clientele.

One night, Debbie and I tried an Italian place where people were lined up outside waiting to get in. I ordered some stuffed mushrooms. They were spoiled, and the rest of the food was just as bad.

I picked at my plate and looked at the line outside.

"If this is the best they've got and I'd open here, we'd be millionaires," I said.

What I didn't know at the time was that most of their clientele wanted soup, salad, entrée, and dessert—for $6.99. At this point in my life, I wasn't going to get out of bed for $6.99.

I closed down the business in my mother's basement, opened a take-out place, and struggled again. Seems like no matter what I did, nothing came easy. I made Debbie quit her job to work with me. The customers in the northeast part of the city weren't used to Italian comfort food, didn't really understand what I was trying to do, and my sandwiches weren't cheap. Quality is never cheap.

I needed a way to make the business work.

With the summer approaching, I decided to sell Italian water ice—a big business in Philly, but only in the summer. A friend of mine owned John's Water Ice in South Philly, and was willing to help me out. We were going to buy the product from John's—a 50-minute round-trip—and sell it at our place.

The night before we were going to start selling the water ice, Debbie woke up in the middle of the night.

"We can't buy it," she said. "We gotta make it ourselves."

"I don't know how to fucking make water ice."

"Let's find out," she said.

We purchased a used water ice machine and then we experimented over the next few days. Within a month, we had the best water ice in northeast Philly with lines around the corner. Customers requested water ice more than food, especially gelati. Not gelato, gelati—layers of water ice, ice cream, and more water ice. We saved $100,000 in one season. I had big plans.

"Let's spend it," I said in January 1987, "and make a nice sit-down restaurant. We'll call it Steve's Italian Kitchen—a nice sit-down place, with takeout and a little window on the side of the building to sell water ice."

Water Ice

>>> Add 3 tablespoons of cherry syrup and 2¾ cups of sugar to 1 gallon of water. Stir, chill, then run through a water ice machine or ice cream machine until the mixture is frozen to a silky texture.

Coming soon to your city, our own famous Martorano's homemade water ice.

I purchased a building that was for sale around the corner from my takeout place. But that black cloud was still hanging around. As soon as we opened, the city closed the street in front of my place for repairs and it almost killed us. I was located in the middle of a street that was ripped up—you couldn't drive up or down the street at all. I needed parking and that traffic, needed people to actually discover us.

Those first couple of months, especially the winter ones, were tough and we just barely made it. Lots of days I'd sit in front of the takeout window and stare out into the cold and gray street. I got down on my knees and prayed a lot, but most importantly I got off my ass and talked up the restaurant around the neighborhood. I'd walk up and down the sidewalks of that ripped up street and talk to whoever would listen, whether I was in front of a funeral home or a pet store, it didn't matter.

Eventually people who loved quality food found us and things were good. I had people dressed in suits and ties waiting in line for a table. Class all the way. We decided to remodel and make the joint into something fancier and change the name to Steve's Ristorante. What was I thinking? We changed the menu and prices to give the place a more upscale feel. But nobody including me knew what a fucking ristorante should be. Big mistakes. No one came. They wanted my old-school food, but I was trying something fancier. With every move I made, I was getting further and further from the things I knew best. A lesson I learned: never forget who you are or where you come from. I wasn't a chef; I was a neighborhood cook.

Left: Steve making his popular sandwiches.

Right: Steve's first restaurant—a take out and delivery place.

CHAPTER 23

When the First Gulf War hit, my business went into the toilet. Oil prices had soared and the economy tanked. Worse, I'd done most of the damage myself. I never had anyone to teach me the business, so much of what I was doing was trial and error. And there were lots of errors, but I wasn't going to cut corners. My mother would scream at me for using quality stuff, but that was the only way I knew.

"You're going to go broke," she'd cry. "What do your customers know about good olive oil? Give them the cheaper stuff. They won't know the difference. Spending all this money—you're like a crazy person."

I tried digging out of the hole, but only made a bigger one by throwing money and credit cards at the problem.

In June of 1991, we closed and said we were remodeling, which was bullshit. To keep money coming in, I sold water ice again—25 and 50 cents a scoop—from the tiny corner of a huge building that was largely empty.

I thought about my father and Anton's. How was selling water ice for quarters any different than pouring shots and beers for the same?

I knew I wasn't a failure—I just had a failed restaurant on my hands. There's really something to that old saying, "location, location, location." It could have happened to anybody. I wasn't going to give up. I decided not to feel sorry for myself and reopen. The new place was going to be like my old business back in my mother's basement and we called it Macaroni's. I was going to sell ravioli, gnocchi, cavatelli, meatballs and chicken cutlets. (In fact, it's still open to this day, with the same name but under different ownership.)

In September 1991, we reopened. Back to basics—and it worked.

Left: The 'Boss' protecting his family!

Right: Some of the products we use at all my restaurants.

CHAPTER 24

I was never a gangster, but many people assumed I was one. Maybe the way I carried myself gave some people a false perception, I don't know. It's true, my family was connected, most of my friends were wiseguys, and many times throughout my life I was headed down that same road. Although what others thought never really bothered me, occasionally it put me in funny situations.

For instance, when my restaurant in northeast Philly wasn't doing well, I had to hustle to make ends meet—loan sharking and doing favors for people. Anyhow, I accumulated about $5,000 and decided to go to Atlantic City with some buddies who hung out at my place. One of the guys named Johnny was a strong, tough kid who loved to quote lines from mob movies like "Goodfellas." He truly believed that I was a made guy.

We drove to the casinos in Atlantic City, and on the way, Johnny kept telling us that he wanted to be "made," wanted to be like us.

"Stop breaking my balls," I said. "We're not gangsters!"

But he didn't believe me. He wouldn't shut up and kept quoting movie lines. Finally, we pulled off on the side of the Atlantic City Expressway, stood him up, pricked his finger, and pulled out a business card that we pretended had an oath written on it. We made him repeat some words in Italian and pronounced Johnny a made man.

"You're with us," I said. "Now shut the fuck up."

We got to Atlantic City and I quickly blew the five grand gambling. I was broke, didn't have money for food or even change for the toll road back. Our new "made man" Johnny had an idea.

"Should I rob a high roller?" he asked.

"No," I shouted, "But it's your job to find us money. So, go look in the car."

Johnny searched the car and eventually found $10 in change in the back seats. We sent him to The White House Steak Shop for a hoagie and drove back to Philadelphia eating and laughing. And the best part was that Johnny thought he was a made guy for weeks after our Atlantic City trip.

Homemade Pizza with Martorano Marinara Sauce & Soppazzada

>>> Buy some pizza dough from your local market. Spread the dough as thin as you'd like with a rolling pin. Open a can of imported San Marzanos and put the tomatoes through a food mill so they are smooth. You can also open a jar of Café Martorano pasta sauce and put that through a food mill if you prefer. Spread the sauce on the dough and season with Kosher salt. Then add grated Parmigiano cheese, fresh basil and slices of your favorite meat (I like soppazzada or pepperoni). You can fry hot peppers in extra-virgin olive oil if you want.

>>> Bake on a pizza stone at 550 until crispy.

artorano's
THE MOVIE
PART I

SECTION 4

Going South

The finishing touch to the Bucatini Carbonara, a fresh egg yolk.

CHAPTER 25

Me and Fat Frankie smuggled the chicken cutlet sandwiches into the visiting room of the prison. Our socks bulged like we had tumors, but the jerk-off guards either didn't notice or care that we were secretly packing Italian comfort food for one of their big shot prisoners.

We had been here before, but by 1991 the trips were becoming more regular when my uncle began to believe his conviction would soon be overturned on appeal.

We unwrapped the sandwiches and pulled up chairs to my uncle. He was wearing an orange jumpsuit like the other inmates, but appeared in control as if he was still in his office at John's Vending. He always shared his food with some of the other wiseguys, friends from New York and Philadelphia, who were also in the visiting room.

"Let me talk with my nephew alone for a few minutes," he said. My uncle signaled for Fat Frankie to take a seat at a nearby table.

"Do something for me," my uncle said.

"Anything you need."

"Deliver a message," he said.

The smoke had begun to clear from the Philly mob war that had started 11 years earlier with the assassination of Angelo Bruno. With blessings from New York, Bruno's former driver John Stanfa had recently been elevated to acting boss of the Philadelphia family, succeeding Nicky Scarfo. But it was still a dangerous time on the streets. Stanfa, a Sicilian from Palermo, was in charge of a family that was deeply divided. A split had developed between the old guard and the sons of former Philly mobsters known as "The Turks."

Uncle Raymond, who had kept his mouth shut during his entire bid, was now wondering what role he would play upon his release. He had been loyal and was expecting the same in return.

He took a bite of the chicken cutlet sandwich and closed his eyes, perhaps thinking of the day he would be set free and no longer had to have his favorite meals delivered in a fucking sweatsock. Then my uncle leaned forward and spoke.

"Ask my friend what the weather is like out on the street," he said, referring to John Stanfa.

I had sunk everything—$170,000—into the place in northeast Philly. The restaurant was my retirement, the money for my kids' education, the cash to take care of my mother. The property was valued at $1.5 million, but because the real estate market was shit, I had recently sold it to two brothers that worked for me as waiters for pennies. I had little left, and now, once again, I was being pulled back into a life I had tried to leave behind. My uncle wanted me to speak with Stanfa.

"You got it," I said.

"Thanks, my nephew."

Stanfa came in to my restaurant once a month for perciatelli with pancetta and onions, and I'd pass along Uncle Raymond's messages to the boss. Most of what was said was in some kind of code, so I never was quite sure what any of it meant, but I had a feeling it wasn't good.

Bucatini Amatriciana—Guanciale and Onions

Mush's favorite.

>>> Take some guanciale and cut it into thin slices. If you can't get guanciale you can substitute pancetta (Italian bacon). Then slice a red onion the same way. Saute some garlic and guanciale together with extra-virgin olive oil. When the guanciale begins to render, add the onions and some crushed red pepper flakes. Cook until the onions are soft. Then add your San Marzano tomatoes and season with Kosher salt, crushed black pepper and fresh basil. When the sauce is done you must use Pecorino-Romano cheese.

Top left: Hand-crushing the San Marzano tomatoes.

Middle: Quality ingredients I use in my restaurants.

Bottom right: The finishing touch- imported Pecorino-Romano cheese.

CHAPTER 26

While I continued to pass messages between Uncle Raymond and Stanfa, Debbie and I worked on our next move.

Philadelphia was our home, but moving to Florida had always been a dream of ours. We decided to visit some friends there and check out the area. Before we left, I put in a call to an old friend, Raymond Abruzzi.

Abruzzi, who years earlier played for the New York Jets and opened the Upper East Side bar Bachelor's III in New York with his old teammate Joe Namath, had moved to Fort Lauderdale and opened another Bachelor's III. I had hoped he was willing to offer some advice.

We booked the trip and stayed with Debbie's girlfriend who lived in Coral Springs, Florida. It was a nice community with good schools and quiet homes a few miles northwest of Fort Lauderdale. It was a great place to raise a family. At night, I drove around to check out the local night-life and look into vacant properties, but by 9 o'clock in the evening, everyone appeared to be ready for bed. You gotta be fucking kidding me. All they had was pizzerias serving so-so Italian food. I needed a restaurant with nightlife and action.

Disappointed and vowing never to come back to Florida, we packed for home. But, before we left, I called Ray and told him Florida wasn't for me.

"Cuz, there's not shit for me here. These people are asleep by fucking 9 o'clock. I'm going back to Philly and do what I got to do."

"Stop being such a jerk-off," Abruzzi said. "Get that South Philly mentality out of your head."

"I got a family, you know? I need to earn."

"Come to Fort Lauderdale and check it out," said Abruzzi. "I happen to know for a fact that there's a little place for you just across from my condo."

On the way to the airport, we stopped by a strip-mall on Oakland Park Blvd and A1A. I looked in the window. It was small—800 square feet or so—but I fell in love. On the spot, we decided to buy the place.

When Debbie and I got back to Philly, I worked the phones and made the deals. I put a down payment on the restaurant and a home.

Attention to details.
Everything has to be perfect.

CHAPTER 27

On my last day in Philadelphia before Debbie and I moved to Florida, I bumped into a kid on the street who told me that "Dutchie" Bracco had been killed.

"Dutchie" was a guy from the neighborhood, one of John Stanfa's soldiers. Stanfa's people had sent the kid out into the streets and bars to see if anyone had been celebrating Bracco's death.

We went to Egypt's, a nightclub on Delaware Avenue. I spotted a friend of mine, Freddie, at the bar with five or six other guys. Freddie had done work for the Greek mafia in Philly and appeared to be having a good time with his new friends.

"Hey, I'm leaving for Florida tomorrow," I said to Freddie. "You didn't call or meet me for dinner, or anything. Where you been? What's the story?"

"Be right with ya. I'm having a business meeting," he said.

I walked away and had a drink at the bar.

Suddenly, a guy wearing a cowboy hat and boots came into the bar and started pointing his finger at Freddie and getting in his face. I rushed over and separated them. The guy pulled out a .44 and put the barrel to my head. Freddie backed up and the rest of the bar went silent.

"Yo, cuz," I said, "you got the gun, I don't."

I backed off, turned to the bartender, and ordered another drink. Freddie's brother, who was on the other side of the bar, rushed over to straighten things out.

"Cuz," said Freddie's brother to the guy wearing the cowboy hat, "put that gun down. Stevie's like family to me."

"You got balls," said the guy as he put away his gun.

"Yeah, like I said, cuz, you have the gun, I don't."

Right then and there, I knew I didn't want that lifestyle. And in 24 hours or so, I'd be in Florida starting my new life—far away from that kind of bullshit.

CHAPTER 28

With my pockets practically empty, I headed to Fort Lauderdale. When everything was said and done, I only had $40 to my name. Forty dollars wasn't going to go far—I wasn't stupid. Crazy, maybe. But my balls were big and I didn't give a fuck. More importantly, I believed in myself.

I knew 90 percent of restaurants failed within a year of opening their doors, and Oakland Park Boulevard in Fort Lauderdale wasn't fucking Broad Street in South Philly. There was no foot-traffic, unless you counted the hookers or the bums that would pass out in the parking lot on their way to the liquor store down the street. A drug store anchored one corner of the shopping center, but the rest of the stores were vacant, except a dry cleaner's and mine.

Inside, the walls were painted in pastels—pinks and blues that made me want to throw up. Eight small tables with plastic pink tablecloths were scattered about, and there was only one fridge, one stove and one pizza oven—and I didn't even make pizza at that time.

Inside the old Café Martorano.

White Pizza with arugula, tomatoes and white truffle oil

I didn't make pizza when I first opened Café Martorano, but I do now and we sell a ton of the stuff.

>>> You can make your own dough if you'd like, but in this day and age, it's so easy to buy a dough ball from a local pizzeria or a pre-made crust from the supermarket.

>>> For the dough, combine 1¾ cup of Caputo pizza flour, 1 teaspoon of yeast, 1 teaspoon of Kosher salt, and 1 teaspoon of extra-virgin olive oil with ¾ of warm water in a bowl. Either use a stand mixer or prep the dough by hand. Cover the dough and let it double in size.

>>> Stretch out the dough to 10 to 12 inches. Sprinkle with garlic powder and Kosher salt then layer with fresh mozzarella, drizzle with extra-virgin olive oil and bake in pre-heated oven until crispy.

>>> Top the hot pizza dough with marinated tomatoes that have been seasoned with garlic powder, Kosher salt, fresh basil and black pepper. Finish with Parmigiano-Reggiano, arugula and drizzle with white truffle oil. If you want, add some Prosciutto Di Parma.

Top: Making one of my homestyle pizzas.

Middle: The tattoo on my right arm. Yo Cuz!

Bottom: Scotty, my wine guy.

YoCuz

Still, I had a good feeling about my new little place in Fort Lauderdale. I believed. I knew it was going to be a success, but it needed a great name. I loved seafood, so I thought about calling it Pescatores. Then I thought about going old-school and calling it Steve's Italian Kitchen. None of the names seemed right, though. I wanted this place to shine like a diamond. Then I thought of my father and uncle and everything our family had been through, and decided that this new restaurant should carry the Martorano name.

And with that, Café Martorano was born.

Next, we needed some rules. Mine. I was the boss and was going to carry this place on my shoulders if that's what it needed to be great. Second, that pink and blue bullshit had to go. What—was Cinderella going to cook here? I was a black-and-white kinda guy, so we painted and put the pink table cloths in the dumpster where they belonged. I didn't give a fuck if those were Florida colors or not; I was from South Philly. Next, I decided that because of our limited resources—I was obviously going to do all of the cooking, Debbie would wait tables, my mother could play hostess, and I had hired a Cuban kid to wash dishes—there weren't going to be any substitutions or special orders. We couldn't afford to put up with that kind of crap, so I let people know where I stood, right on bottom of the menu in black and white we printed: NO SUBSTITUTIONS. DON'T BREAK BALLS. And, most importantly, I was going to stay true to myself. This wasn't going to be a ristorante —whatever the fuck that was. I'd made that mistake before. Not this time. Café Martorano was going to be all me—from the heart. I was going to serve the dishes I grew up with and cook like Frank Sinatra sang—my way.

The Cuban kid didn't last long. A short time after we opened, he got arrested. I bailed him out and never saw him again. I tried washing dishes and cooking for awhile, but that was too much. So, I put a sign in the window and hoped for the best. A day or two later, a thin guy wearing bright red suspenders, a white T-shirt and a pair of old jeans came in carrying the sign. He said his name was Angel. He had come from San Francisco looking for work.

"Jesus Christ, look at you," I said, staring at his bright red suspenders. "Cuz, how the fuck am I supposed to work with you looking like that?"

"Give me a chance," he said. "I'm a hard worker. You won't be sorry, I promise."

A guy named Angel from San Francisco? That's all I need, a finoccio, I thought. But I was wrong on two accounts. One, the guy was a helluva ladies man, and two, he stood with me, and now 18 years later, he's the best of the best: My angel on my shoulder. He always, always has my back.

EXTRAS

Homemade Gnocchi /12 Risotto /12 Sautéed Greens /10
Truffle Fries /12 Mac n Cheese /16

ABSOLUTELY NO CHANGES OR SUBSTITUTIONS. Just let me do what I do and don't break balls.
20% GRATUITY WILL BE ADDED TO PARTIES OF 6 OR MORE

The bottom of my menu tells the story of my success. Taste my food my way, you will fall in love and come back for more.

Café Martorano's elegant sign with Steve's signature logo.

My head waiter, Angel. He's my angel on my shoulder. He's been with me for 18 years.

CHAPTER 29

After our first week, I needed to go out and spend money with bartenders and cocktail waitresses, so they would come and give me a play. I asked Debbie for $20 from the register.

She resisted.

"I know what I'm doin'," I said, "just gimme $20."

Although he wasn't a big spender, my father always believed that money could buy a lot of goodwill. "Son," he used to say, "go out and take care of the bartenders and waitresses at the other places in your neighborhood, and I promise they'll take care of you."

"I know what I'm doin'," I said again to Debbie. "Just gimme the fucking money. It's going to be OK."

In truth, it wasn't OK. At least yet. After buying the restaurant and the house, we didn't even have money left for furniture. Debbie, me and our two boys, Joey and Steven, were sleeping on the floor. When we watched TV or ate, we sat on plastic beach chairs. The only real furniture in the house belonged to my mother; we had shipped her bedroom set from Philly to South Florida. I wasn't about to let my mother sleep on the floor. I also wasn't going to see this restaurant fail. Twenty dollars wasn't going to hurt, and I knew that if we got in trouble, we always had the credit cards.

"We're gonna be OK," I said again.

I drove a few blocks up the street to a high-end restaurant and nightclub called Septembers and ordered the cheapest thing I could find, a $3 glass of white wine. I nursed the drink for all that it was worth, then tipped the bartender the remaining $17.

"This for me?" he said. "Thanks."

"No problem," I said. "But could you do me a favor?"

"Name it."

"I just opened a little Italian-American place down the street. It's all comfort food. I'm from South Philly and I'm the cook, so stop by for a free glass of wine."

"Be glad to," said my new friend. "And while you're here, you should talk to the other bartender over there." He pointed across the room. "He's from Philly, too."

I talked to the Philly guy and finished my drink, then went to the bathroom and filled my wine glass with water from the tap because I had no money left for another drink. I went back out into the bar and kept my hand over my glass so know one would notice that I was drinking water instead of wine. And I told anyone who'd listen:

"You gotta try Café Martorano, the best Italian-American cooking in the world. And, yeah, I'm from South Philly."

CHAPTER 30

A few months after I opened Café Martorano, I was working out in the gym and got a phone call from the restaurant.

"You'll never guess who wants to eat at the restaurant tonight," said one of my guys. "Tony Bennett!"

"Get the fuck out," I said. "Tony Bennett?"

"I know, I know! Can you believe that? He's in town for a concert or something. I spoke with one his assistants."

"That's fucking unbelievable."

"There's just one thing—they're looking for some kind of deal."

"A what?"

Apparently, when Bennett would come to Fort Lauderdale, he usually ate at an Italian place just up the street from us and the owner would give Bennett and his entire entourage half-price on the bar and other free stuff. It wasn't an unusual request; some celebrities tried to pull that kind of shit all of the time. But I didn't have a full bar—just wine and beer—and I certainly wasn't in a position to give anything away. What pissed me off, though, was that we were probably dealing with some kind of jerk-off assistant, not Bennett himself. I figured Bennett gave him something like $1,000 to find a place to eat and the assistant was trying to find a deal and pocket the rest.

"Tell this assistant guy that Tony Bennett and his group can go the fuck up the street because I just opened and can't afford to give shit away," I said. "Then tell that motherfucker that the next time Tony Bennett is in town, he should give our entourage free tickets to his show. See how he likes that."

After working out, I did all my food shopping and went back to the restaurant.

"Bennett's people called back. They still want to come in."

The picture of my first celebrity, Tony Bennett, hangs in Café Martorano to this day.

I was surprised, but also excited. This was a first for me. I'd cooked for wiseguys before, but never a celebrity. I washed my hands, headed for the kitchen, and went to work.

About an hour later, I stepped into the dining room and walked past an old man and his group. One member of the group got up from their table and grabbed me by the arm.

"Steve, right?" said the guy. "You wanna meet Tony Bennett?"

"Yeah, where is he?"

I'd just walked past him and didn't even notice.

Tony Bennett stood up and extended his hand. "I'm excited about eating here," he said.

"I'm excited about cooking for you."

Bennett had a concert that night and was eating light, so I went to the kitchen and prepared orecchiette with broccoli rabe, no sausage.

Tony Fucking Bennett, I thought as I cooked. In my restaurant!

He was my first celebrity, but he wouldn't be the last.

Orecchiette with Broccoli Rabe

>>> Smash and finely chop a couple of garlic cloves and brown the garlic in a pan with some extra-virgin olive oil and a touch of red pepper flakes, some kosher salt, and some anchovy (if you like). At this point, you can also add and brown a few sliced links of Italian sausage (I use a mix of hot and sweet). Cook the macaroni in a pot with some lightly salted water. Three minutes before the macaroni is finished, add the broccoli rabe (recipe on page 45) to the pot. Take a tablespoon or so of the macaroni/rabe water and add it the oil mixture. Then drain the macaroni and rabe, add it to the pan with the oil. Toss in some chopped Italian parsley and some toasted bread crumbs.

CHAPTER 31

By 1997, five years after we first opened, things couldn't have been better. We expanded next door. We knocked down the wall and added another 800-square-feet, nearly doubling our space. I upgraded our house stereo, trading our old CD player for a DJ booth. Then I outfitted the restaurant with TVs, big-ass speakers, Martin lights, and, of course, a mirror ball. I started showing movies just like I had at Anton's and was spinning records again like I did in my glory days at Valentino's in Cherry Hill.

Everything was big, bold, and loud—even the meatballs I served. It was South Philly in South Florida. My place had finally taken on my personality. And Café Martorano went from being a hidden gem to having a line every single night.

That same year former quarterback Joe Montana even asked me to cook for the first annual charity benefit hosted by his Four Rings Foundation. Joe was an idol of mine, so I was thrilled to have the chance to help him out.

I had gotten to know Joe and his family through Warren Greene, who was the agent for the star quarterback and others including Pete Rose and Shaquille O'Neal. Joe wanted to have me and a three-man crew out to his estate for a weekend in Napa Valley. He asked if I was interested in cooking for his kids (they loved my pizza and cheesesteaks) and later for a charity event at the MacMurray Ranch, a winery once owned by Fred MacMurray, the famous actor who appeared in movies and on TVs "My Three Sons" and had passed away in 1991.

The deal was to cook for about 800 people in addition to Joe's family beforehand. I hadn't done anything like that before, but I jumped at the chance.

Joe arrived at the airport on Friday to pick us up just as the sun began to set, and by the time we got to his place it was pitch dark. As we drove along, I could tell we were going up a mountain, but I couldn't see a thing and was nervous because I had to pull this off.

Steve with Joe Montana at his Napa Valley Home.

"Joe, if a guy had a couple drinks in him, he'd go right off the edge, wouldn't he?" I asked, making sure my seat belt was tight. He laughed, but kept on climbing the mountain in his truck until we arrived at the estate, safe and sound.

The house was gorgeous. Inspired by a trip to Italy, Joe and his wife outfitted their place in Italian marble and furniture. It seemed as if everything he owned, including the wood beams in the high ceilings, had been imported from Italy.

When the tour concluded, Joe pointed us to the guest house. Still dark, and I still couldn't see a thing.

"Watch out for snakes," he joked. "And don't fall off the side of the mountain."

The next morning I cooked for Joe's kids on a patio that overlooked a valley. It was hard to believe: an Italian guy from South Philly in California cooking for Joe Montana's family and friends. It felt like a dream and I didn't want to wake up.

Afterward, we headed to the ranch and prepared for the main event. When I reached the kitchen I stopped cold. The room was probably in the same condition in which it was when it was built in the late 1950s or early 1960s. It was as tiny as a closet and had only an old four-burner stove. Fred MacMurray had been one of my favorites as a kid and the guy certainly knew how to act, but his old kitchen was shit.

I looked at Joe and he shrugged.

"Sorry," he said. "I had no idea."

I told Joe not to worry about it and went to work. I started out cooking in my mother's basement on a four-burner stove, so I made myself at home. We made use of a barbeque pit and some grills outside, and fired up the old stove in the outdated kitchen. Somehow we managed to get by. Hours later, I stepped out of the kitchen and took a look outside.

Hundreds of well-dressed people were seated on long tables with crisp, white tablecloths trimmed with black bows. They were all drinking wine, eating and enjoying themselves. As the sun began to set, the light danced on the mountains in the background. I had never seen anything so beautiful in my life. This setting, all these people eating my food—it was unbelievable. It was the same stuff I grew up eating. I was proud to be a Martorano from South Philly. It almost seemed like an ending to a movie, but it was just a beginning.

CHAPTER 32

The next year, during the summer of 1998, I went to New York on a business trip and wound up having dinner with a couple of "fellas."

I had known some of these fellas from my early days in Florida, but I'd been out of that world for some time and wanted to keep it that way. Still, I didn't want to insult anyone, so when they suggested meeting over dinner to talk a little business, I figured it couldn't hurt and needed to give them their respect.

At the restaurant, one of the fellas said he was glad that we were friends, but thought our relationship needed to get a little stronger. They'd been paying attention to Café Martorano, seen it grow and become a success, and wanted to play a part in helping me in the future.

I told them thanks, but that this was something I should probably talk over with my uncle, who was still away. I also reminded them that they were from New York and I was from Philly, a fact that made me uncomfortable. Plus, I was doing just fine on my own with help from no one.

I went back to Florida and waited for a call from Uncle Raymond. I told him I had a problem. He told me not to worry about anything. My uncle was going to get a message to the guys, so I figured that was that.

A few months later, in December, a couple of no-neck guys wearing suits came into Café Martorano looking for me.

"Steve, got a minute?" one of them asked. "Is there somewhere we can talk?"

We went to a back room of the restaurant and I closed the door.

"We're here to pick up our Christmas present," said one of the men.

"Your what?" I said. I was stunned.

"Our Christmas present," the man repeated. "You know, $25,000."

I said: "I don't have that kind of money. And even if I did, I'm not giving it away. Now, I gotta go back and cook. You can stick around if you want—there's a couple of aprons over there." Now my balls were twisted.

The two men looked at one another and smiled.

"We'll be back next week and see what you say then," said the guy who had been doing all of the talking.

They left and I caught my breath. I thought, what the fuck was that about?

I got a message to my uncle in prison. He sent me a message about what to do. He told me to reach out to "that friend of ours" in New York and tell him what had happened, so I did.

"What should I do if they come back?" I asked.

"Tell them guys they're gonna have to kill you and then come and kill me because they ain't getting a fucking dime," said my uncle. "Then tell them I'll be home real soon."

As promised, the men came back a week later. I was sweating my balls off from cooking, but I stood firm and delivered the message to those fellas.

"My uncle said for you to kill me and then kill him because you ain't getting nothing."

"That's a real possibility," said one of the men.

They left and I never saw them again. To this day, that friendship with that friend of ours in New York means a lot.

Left: I have the most loyal kitchen crew, been together for 18 years.

CHAPTER 33

Uncle Raymond was released from prison in November 1999 when his conviction was overturned. He spent 17 years in prison.

Shortly after he became a free man, we held a homecoming party for him at Café Martorano. The night my uncle walked through that door with my Aunt Evelyn, it was like a celebrity had come to the restaurant. He had done a long stretch and didn't rat on anyone, staying true to the things he believed in. Everyone was excited and in the mood to celebrate, but we kept things low key. At the end of the night, we sat down together and had a drink.

"I'm very proud of you, my nephew," he said.

Caesar Salad

>>> For the dressing, put eight anchovy fillets, eight garlic gloves, eight egg yolks and 8 tablespoons of Dijon mustard in a blender and mix until emulsified. Fold 2 cups of grated Parmesan into the dressing and chill.

>>> For the garlic croutons, slice some Filone or other Italian bread into cubes. In a pan, heat 8 ounces of butter with 1 ounce of granulated garlic powder, a pinch of freshly chopped Italian parsley and Kosher salt to taste. When the butter is melted, add the Filone cubes and allow the bread to soak up the mixture. Remove the cubes from the pan and toast them on a sheet pan in the oven.

>>> For the greens, we use 4 cups of chopped romaine. Toss the greens with the croutons and the dressing then serve.

Penne with Vodka Sauce

>>> In a sauce pan brown the diced pancetta. When crispy, add chopped onion, crushed red pepper flakes, add a little vodka, then add San Marzano tomatoes. Cook for 10 minutes, add heavy cream, Italian parsley and freshly grated Parmigiano-Reggiano cheese.

Lobster Franchese

This one is for Fat Joe—it's his favorite.

>>> De-shell a lobster tail and season it with Kosher salt, crushed black pepper and granulated garlic. Coat the tail with flour, then dredge in an egg wash seasoned with some grated Parmesan, Kosher salt, crushed black pepper, Italian parsley and granulated garlic. Bring about a $\frac{1}{4}$ cup of vegetable oil in pan to medium-high heat and cook the lobster until golden brown on both sides. Remove the lobster and discard the oil, then return the pan to the heat and add 1 ounce of white wine, 2 ounces of chicken stock, 3 ounces of butter coated in flour, some Italian parsley and a few squeezes of juice from a Meyer lemon. Stuff the lobster with 2 ounces of jumbo lump crab meat. Serve the lobster under a bed of Arborio rice and spoon the pan sauce over the dish.

He spent the next few years traveling and visiting with family.

In early January 2002, someone got to Uncle Raymond while he was driving in his Lincoln Town Car to an appointment in Philadelphia. A gunman put three bullets through the windshield, hitting my uncle in the arm, chest and stomach. That tough son of a bitch Raymond tried driving himself to the hospital with half of his arm hanging off while he was bleeding his guts out.

When I heard the news, I was in the hospital in Fort Lauderdale with my mother, who had broken both of her legs after being hit by a car. (Who else has parents that both get their legs broken and have to learn to walk again?) Raymond was in critical condition. We were told to keep away for our own safety. All I could do was sit, wait, and pray.

I wasn't sure if Uncle Raymond was planning a comeback or not, and have no idea who shot him or why. Sadly, this was a result of the life he chose.

A few weeks after he was shot, Uncle Raymond passed away. He was 74.

When I got the call, I went into the bathroom of my mother's hospital room and looked in the mirror. *Uncle Raymond did his time, kept his mouth shut, and this was the fucking thanks he got?* I knew this was the life he chose, and I reminded myself that I wasn't my uncle. I loved him like a father, but I was making the Martorano name into a legitimate success. I knew what I wanted and, more importantly, what I had to do.

My DJ booth in the kitchen where I spin, play movies and plate the food.

These words that are tattooed on my arm got me through the toughest times of my life.

SECTION 5

It ain't about how hard you hit.

CHAPTER 34

The first step toward taking Café Martorano to the big-time came in 2003. With business booming, we expanded to a third storefront. The night before we closed for renovations, my friend, rapper Fat Joe, was in the restaurant and put on a mini-concert for our guests. He's a big fan of both my chicken wings with mac-n-cheese and lobster franchese, so much so that at the end of his song "Get It Poppin," he gives a shout out to Café Martorano. In another, called "Jealousy," he says, "Yo, Stevie! Martorano, pour that Cristal. Spill that shit, man." After closing, I handed him a sledgehammer and we went to work tearing out a wall so Café Martorano could grow.

The Mother Ship. Café Martorano in Fort Lauderdale.

Chicken Wings with Bibzy-style Sauce

>>> Get 5 pounds of chicken wings and some oyster sauce, which you can find in the Asian section of any grocery store. You'll also need some garlic and sweet chili sauce. Coat the chicken wings with flour seasoned with Kosher salt and crushed black pepper. Fry the wings in a saute pan so they get nice and crisp. Remove the wings and pour the oyster sauce into the saute pan. Add a cup or so of chicken stock or chicken broth until the oyster sauce thins out a bit. Add a little bit of crushed red pepper flakes, a couple cloves of chopped garlic, chili sauce and some green onions or scallions. Return the wings to the pan and get everything moving. Serve them hot and get ready: They'll be back for more.

Martorano Mac-n-Cheese

Like a lot of my recipes, this one is simple, but people go nuts for it.

>>> Bring a quart of heavy cream to a simmer, then add 4 ounces of Velveeta cheese, 4 ounces of provolone, 4 ounces of fontina and 4 ounces of white cheddar. In the meantime, boil a box of macaroni until al dente. Stir the cheese sauce until it's completely melted and combine with the drained macaroni.

>>> You can bring this dish up a few notches by topping it with a couple of handfuls of crispy pancetta and/or toasted bread crumbs or peas.

In honor of my good friend, actress Gabriel Union

DADDY'S
LITTLE GIRLS

Sheer willpower, doing our best every single night, and word of mouth is what got us to that point. It sure as hell didn't happen because of our advertising or because of our customer service; we hardly ever answered the phone and never, never took out ads.

Still, people found us, particularly celebrities. I knew some people who worked at Turnberry Isle, a luxury resort in North Miami Beach that caters to the rich and famous. Every once in awhile, they'd send some of their guests our way, and they'd inevitably end up having a great time. They'd tell their friends about Café Martorano and so on and so on. Really, it was as simple as that.

James Caan—the great actor who played Sonny Corleone in "The Godfather" and did a million other terrific things—was one of those early celebrity patrons of Café Martorano.

I'll never forget the first time he walked through our door sometime in 2002. I'll never forget because—just like the Tony Bennett incident a few years earlier—I didn't even recognize him at first. My mom, who was working as a hostess at the time, came up to me full of excitement and pointed to a man at the bar who looked like Captain Ahab from Moby Dick. (I later discovered Caan's new "look" was for a part in a movie.)

"That's James Caan," she said.

"Nah, ma," I said, "That don't look anything like Sonny Corleone."

I took another longer look, realized my mother was right, and introduced myself. We talked about films and he told me his favorite role was Frank in "Thief," not Sonny in "The Godfather." A few days later, he sent me a signed "Thief" poster to hang in the restaurant. It was the beginning of a great friendship and Jimmy became a regular (his favorite dishes are chicken cacciatore and calamari).

Bibzy Style Galamod.

Fried Galamod-Red

You might call it calamari, we call it galamod in South Philly. No matter how you pronounce it, it's great stuff.

>>> Cut 8 ounces of calamari (white part only) into little rings or tubes. Season with granulated garlic, Kosher salt and crushed black pepper, then coat with flour. Deep fry in a heavy pan for about 3 minutes at 350 degrees, or until the galamod are golden brown.

>>> Serve with a pepper gravy.

>>> For the pepper gravy, dice six red and yellow bell peppers, three hot peppers, three garlic cloves and one white onion. Heat a few ounces of extra-virgin olive oil in a pan, then saute the diced vegetables and season with Kosher salt, crushed black pepper and garlic powder. Add one can of hand-crushed San Marzano tomatoes to the pan and a few basil leaves.

>>> When the gravy is cooked through, serve with the galamod, and garnish with some balsamic vinegar and seasoned bread crumbs.

Chicken Cacciatore

Cacciatore just means hunter style, so this is one of those rustic, peasant dishes.

You'll want to go to a butcher and ask him to take apart a 3-pound chicken. I like cooking with dark meat (that's where the taste comes from), so just hang on to to those breasts and use them for cutlets.

>>> Pat the chicken dry, then season heavily with Kosher salt, crushed black pepper and granulated garlic. Heat a deep frying pan with 1/4 cup of vegetable oil and when the pan is hot add the chicken. Don't touch it. Let it get nice and brown. Then do the other side. It should take about 12 minutes. Remove the chicken and get rid of the oil. Return the pan to the stove and add 1/4 cup of extra-virgin olive oil and eight cloves of smashed garlic. Slice two bell peppers (one red, one yellow), a red onion, and 2 cups of mushrooms (button or assorted) and add those to the pan. Once everything is nice and brown, deglaze the pan with a little dry white wine.

>>> Return the chicken to the pan and add 3 cups of chicken stock. To make this dish red, add a can of hand-crushed San Marzano tomatoes. To keep it white, add another cup or so of stock.

>>> Bring the pan to medium-high heat and let it simmer for 20 minutes. Then pop the lid on and stick it in an oven for 15 minutes at 350 degrees. Once the chicken starts to fall off the bone, it's done, cuz.

CHAPTER 35

It wasn't long before we had people in the parking lot waiting for a table. Even celebrities had to wait their turn. One time Madonna left in a huff because we had a packed house and a three-hour wait. I didn't have the heart to tell her that the reason she couldn't be seated was because another celebrity with an entourage had beaten her to the punch: Steven Tyler of Aerosmith.

One night word got back to the kitchen that the late, great Bruno Kirby was in the parking lot with Linda, his wife, waiting for a table. (Loved him as young Clemenza in "The Godfather II.") I used to feel guilty that I only had a dozen or so tables in the restaurant then, so in order to make the wait for a table a little more bearable I'd send out free appetizers to the customers outside in line. That night Bruno and Linda were in line, I sent out some of my famous meatballs, even though the couple were vegetarians and told me they hadn't eaten meat in something like 10 years.

"Well, that's it," Bruno said. "I'm no longer a vegetarian. I just had to have one—and then another. The best meatball I've ever had."

We even took a picture of him eating it on the hood of a car. Later, after he came in and had dinner, he stayed and listened to me play some Sinatra.

Three stages of a meatball.

"I'm about the biggest fan of Sinatra that there is," Bruno told me.

"I don't think so," I said, "I'm a much bigger fan."

"Prove it," said Bruno.

At that, I removed my shirt and showed him the tattoo of Frank Sinatra on my shoulder.

"You win," he said.

Sometimes when actors came to Café Martorano, I'd play one of their movies while they ate.

A friend of mine sent in Danny DeVito and his wife Rhea Perlman one night. I played "Hoffa" and DeVito's eyes never left the TV screen. When the film ended, I played some disco and Perlman (Carla from the great TV show "Cheers") danced her ass off with the other customers to Gloria Gaynor's "I Will Survive." They must have had a good time. The next day they sent my friend an e-mail to thank him for recommending Café Martorano and told him it was the best Italian food they'd ever had.

Some celebrities want a little less fanfare, and I understand that.

The first time Chazz Palminteri (who wrote and starred in "A Bronx Tale") came in, he made it a point to ask me, "Please, I don't want to see myself while I'm eating here." The second, third and fourth times when he came in for dinner, he said the same thing. Then, one day he showed up after he had finished doing a movie in Florida called "Push."

"Hey, Steve, play whatever you want," he called out; "and for Christ's sake, bring me something marvelous to eat!"

I threw on "Boss of Bosses," and "A Bronx Tale."

And, as you can imagine, some celebrities were a pain.

Frank Sinatra Jr. used to be a customer and always seemed to have special requests. I don't do special requests. Once, we had a disagreement when I refused to make him an order of rigatoni with clams. (I make things the way I make them because they work. I can't promise a dish will be any good if a customer decides to play chef and makes substitutions and additions to a dish. You only serve clams with linguine or a long and thin cut of macaroni, not rigatoni. End of fucking story.)

About a week later, someone at the Hard Rock Casino called and said they were sending over Sinatra Jr. with a rather large group and asked if they could be seated immediately. Oh, boy, I thought, here we go. Reluctantly, we reserved several tables for the group. It was early—around 5 p.m. or so—and we weren't too crowded at that point. But then, they showed up an hour late. As the group was finally seated, I brought out a round of

Top: Neighborhood Tattoo artist, Damien Bart, perfecting Sinatra on me.

Middle: Classic music by Sinatra

appetizers (on the house) and went back into the kitchen, I wanted to get these guys in and out with as little drama as possible.

Sinatra Jr., however, had other ideas.

Fifteen minutes after being seated, Sinatra got up and announced that the music was too loud. He and the group walked out the door without so much as a thank you. He won't be coming back.

Another joining Sinatra on the banned list is Liza Minnelli.

Actually, she started out as a sweetheart, a pretty good customer who ordered a lot of carryout. Then she got sick and was in and out of the hospital. For whatever reason—I guess out of respect and appreciation for her patronage—I'd occasionally send her soup, chicken and salads while she was recuperating. She never said thanks or responded in any kind of way, so I said, fuck it, and let it go.

After she recovered, she made sort of a career comeback, and started coming to Café Martorano again. Once, she showed up at the restaurant in a wheelchair, so we seated her right way. After her meal, however, she managed to get up and walk outside for a cigarette. In her honor, I had been playing a video of Judy Garland (her mother), Frank Sinatra and Dean Martin doing some kind of performance. After her cigarette break, Liza Minnelli stopped at the hostess table and asked my mother about the video.

"Where'd he get it?" she asked "Did he steal that from my father?"

"My son doesn't steal," said my mother.

When my mother told me what had happened, I kicked out Ms. Minnelli and told that bitch to never come back.

Steve's Comfort Soup

This is comfort soup on a cold day.

>>> Warm up a few cups of chicken broth or stock. Make a little pastina. Throw it in the soup with a little Italian parsley and some grated Parmesan.

Of course, in true Steve Martorano style, we played movies at our Grand Opening at the Rio in Las Vegas.

CHAPTER 36

In 2003, the Foxwoods Resort Casino in Connecticut asked me to cook at a big event featuring the cast of "The Sopranos." It was kind of a tribute night for Foxwoods' high rollers. They sent out something like 800 invitations.

I had never cooked for that many people before, especially out of a kitchen other than my own. A lot of the people from Boston, Chicago and New York didn't just come to the Foxwood event for the Sopranos—they came for us, for our cooking.

We had a private dinner for the cast, and I took a half-wheel of Parmagiano-Reggiano (the best) and cut it in half. A wheel like that weighed 50 or 60 pounds and cost $800. I removed the cheese and grated it. Then I made rigatoni with a Sunday pork gravy, pigs' feet, spare ribs, meatballs, and threw the macaroni and everything into the wheel of cheese. I finished it off with ricotta, and put it in the middle of the table. James Gandolfini, Tony Soprano himself, went nuts; he loved it.

I must have made a good impression. I was invited back to cook for the following year's high rollers event, and Tony Sirico, who played Paulie Walnuts on "The Sopranos" invited me and my boys up to New Jersey to cook for a fundraiser for the Marlo Thomas Foundation. We cooked for about 550 people. Before dinner, James Gandolfini said he was starving. So, while cooking for the crowd, I made him some perciatelli with pancetta and onions.

After those events, a lot of the cast members started coming down to my place in Fort Lauderdale to eat. Steven Van Zandt ("Little Stevie" from Bruce Springsteen's band who also played Silvio Dante, the consigliore, on "The Sopranos") loves to come to Café Martorano. He won't eat seafood, but he always orders three entrees every time, like ravioli, veal piccata and penne with cognac. Frankie Vincent who played Phil Leotardo on "The Sopranos" loves my shrimp scampi bread. Lorraine Bracco, who co-starred in "Goodfellas" and played psychiatrist Jennifer Melfi on "The Sopranos," loves my eggplant stack.

Penne with Cognac

I like to use penne macaroni here, but you can use rigatoni or pennoni macaroni, which is a larger version of penne. This one is Steve Van Zandts' favorite. Van Zandt is a legend as a musician and actor in "The Sopranos."

>>> In a sauce pan brown the diced pancetta. When crispy, add chopped onion, crushed red pepper flakes, add a little Cognac, then add San Marzano tomatoes. Cook for 10 minutes, add heavy cream, Italian parsley and fresh grated Parmigiano-Reggiano cheese.

Shrimp Scampi Bread

>>> De-vein and clean two jumbo shrimp then get some clam broth. Cook up a dozen Cherry Stone clams. Get some olive oil, garlic, crushed red pepper and a little white wine then put it in a pot and cover. That's your stock. You can chop up the clams to use for something else—we just want the broth. You can use bottled clam broth, but it's not going to be the same. Put some extra-virgin olive oil in a pan with two to three cloves of garlic. Saute the shrimp until they get pink. Throw in some white wine, Kosher salt, crushed black pepper and garlic powder. Add the clam broth and some Italian parsley. Chop up one tomato for color. Add a handful of frozen peas (not canned). Add some lightly salted butter, and cover for 2 or 3 minutes until the shrimp is done. Pour it over toasted bread, and you're done.

Eggplant Stack

>>> You will need one large eggplant, a little Kosher salt and crushed black pepper to taste, a cup of Progresso seasoned bread crumbs (or homemade seasoned bread crumbs), two eggs, $1/2$ cup of flour, 1 cup of vegetable oil for frying and 1 pound of fresh cow mozzarella (not buffalo mozzarella). The mozzarella should be bought in an Italian deli, not in a supermarket.

>>> Slice the eggplant longways. Salt the eggplant on each side and put it in a colander to drain for about 30 minutes to get the excess bitterness out. Make an egg wash using the egg, salt, pepper, a little Italian parsley and some grated cheese. Dip the eggplant slices into the flour and then into the egg mixture and then into the bread crumbs. Repeat with the rest of the eggplant slices.

>>> Heat the oil in the skillet, and fry the eggplant slices until they get crisp and golden brown. Don't crowd the pan. Do two or three slices at a time. Take them out and let them drain on a paper towel to get the excess oil off. Put the eggplant slices on a plate. Slice tomatoes, season with Kosher salt, crushed black pepper, extra-virgin olive oil, balsamic vinegar and basil and place them on top of the eggplant. Add a few slices of mozzarella on top. Repeat the process. After two stacks, toss arugula that has been cleaned and dried with salt and pepper and extra-virgin olive oil then add it to the stack. Add a little more extra-virgin olive oil and balsamic vinegar. Add a little Parmigiano-Reggiano cheese on top.

Lorraine likes to come back into the kitchen, too. The first time she ventured behind the line, it was like seeing her in Martin Scorsese's famous long tracking shot from "Goodfellas," when Henry Hill takes her by the hand through the Copacabana Night Club. The guys on staff were all quoting movie lines to her, and the restaurant erupted when Lorraine responded in kind. "You've got some nerve," she said. "Standing me up. Who do you think you think you are? Frankie Valli or some kind of big shot?"

Top: The kitchen line.

Bottom: Café Martorano's jarred sauces.

CHAPTER 37

One night in 2005, we had a nice crowd, but were not overly busy, and seven people walked in. They asked me to cook for them. I approached the table, and I gave my spiel.

"The stuff you get here, you're not gonna get anywhere else. I'll start you out with a Philly cheesesteak—homestyle, like my mother would make—and some chicken wings done in a special sauce that will blow your minds. Then, we'll go with an Italian hoagie, a pizza and, of course, my meatballs."

"Just keep the food coming," they said.

After the appetizers and about three macaroni dishes, they threw in the towel.

"We're done!" they said.

I found out later that the guy who brought in the group was Marvin Shankman, the owner and publisher of Cigar Aficionado and the Wine Spectator magazines. Later, he sent me a letter that said, "It would be an honor for me to write an article about Café Martorano in Cigar Aficionado. Do you mind if I send a photographer?"

To me, that was a big deal. I later found out that Shankman never did reviews, so I was touched that he picked Café Martorano for his first. Great article. Great publicity. Stuff like that really helped put us on the map. We've had a lot of reviews over the years—and, to tell the truth, most of them get my balls twisted for one reason or another—but I appreciated the Cigar Aficionado review because the guy who wrote it really knew food. A couple of years later, we got another great plug when a writer from Gourmet magazine wrote, "[Steve Martorano] may just make the best meatball in the world."

Public praise and good reviews from respected writers are great, but honestly nothing means more to me than when someone from the old neighborhood comes in and says, "My mom's was good, but yours is better."

My Mom and me in front of The Godfather— An Italian-American Classic.

CHAPTER 38

One of our biggest celebrity customers—literally the biggest—is Shaquille O'Neal. I got tight with Shaq when he came from the Lakers to the Miami Heat in 2004 and would come into Café Martorano and order fettuccine alfredo for dinner and ask for another plate for dessert.

Pappardelle with Parmigiana Cream Sauce

Shaq calls it fettuccine alfredo, but it's really pappardelle with parmigiana cream sauce. Either way, he loves it and so does everyone else.

In Italy, they don't even make it with cream. In Italy, it's made with butter. But I've never been to Italy. All these guys act like they're from Italy, so they can let the public think they cook like Italians. I've never been there, so why would I want to cook like that? Let them do what they do, and I'll do what I do.

>>> Take a large sauce pan and fill it half-way with heavy cream and a tablespoon of butter, then reduce it by half. A little Kosher salt, crushed black pepper, and some great Parmigiano-Reggiano cheese, and that's it.

In 2006, the Heat won the NBA Championship. Steve Stowe, a Heat executive and mutual friend of mine and Shaq, came into Café Martorano shortly after the Heat won the title.

"Don't say anything," Stowe told me, "but Shaq wants to get you a championship ring as a surprise. What's your ring size?"

I was humbled and excited. What cook in the world gets an honor like that, I thought.

Weeks passed. Then months. Shaq stopped coming into the restaurant, and then I forgot about the ring.

Then one night I ran into one of Shaq's teammates, Eddie Jones. He told me that Shaq was just pulling a prank, that the ring was a joke.

"I can't believe you fell for that," said Jones. "He does that to everyone."

A few more weeks passed, and Shaq finally came back to Café Martorano. I was in the DJ booth that night, grabbed the microphone, and gave him a hard time.

"Get outta here," I joked. "You're not wanted."

"Didn't you get my present, Steve?" Shaq asked.

"What present?"

Shaq looked hurt and was quiet for the rest of the night.

A few nights later, Steve Stowe came into the restaurant with his family and told me that Shaq was coming in again, too. Sure enough, Shaq appeared at the door with that famous smile and a small box. We walked into the back office and Shaq gave me a championship ring. Eddie Jones was the one who had been pulling my leg, not Shaq.

Shaq eating at CaféMartorano.

“We’re a lot alike,” said Shaq. “I’m great for what I do, you’re great for what you do, and we both make people happy.”

Two rings were given to me: one by Ludacris on his 30th birthday for friendship, and the other by Shaq when he won the championship with the Miami Heat.

CHAPTER 39

I've never done this for the money. I really don't even respect money. If you have it, you have it, and that's great, I guess. But the stuff is never really yours, and when you die it's going to be left to someone else. Money can be taken away.

Passion, on the other hand, can't. I'll take passion over money any fucking day of the week. And, the best part is that if you have a passion for something and follow your heart, I'm telling ya, cuz, good things are going to come. But, here's the trick: You have to believe in yourself.

Look at me. Let's be honest here. I'm not a smart guy. School wasn't a big thing for me. I didn't have interest in a whole a lot of stuff except food, music and movies. But the biggest problem was that my hand was pretty much dealt on the day I was born. Growing up a Martorano in South Philly meant everyone expected that I was either going to drive a truck like my father or get pinched and go to jail like my uncle and cousin. Long John was a wiseguy whose business was making money any way he could. I'm not ashamed of that. He did what he had to do and didn't sit around taking welfare. I'm proud of my family and where I come from. I make no judgments. But, like it or not, the name was infamous.

My goal was always to rebrand the name Martorano and have people associate it with a knock-your-fucking-socks-off dining experience. Since day one, that had always been my passion, but I knew if I was going to make that happen, I was going have to be the best.

In 2007 came the one opportunity I'd been waiting for my whole life, that chance to be the best: Vegas, the fucking big league.

It was almost the end of me.

My first restaurant in Las Vegas

CHAPTER 40

In early 2007 I brought a group of my guys from South Florida to Vegas to start a second Café Martorano at the Rio Hotel and Casino. The space was huge—about 7,000 square feet—and located in the back of the casino. Even though two restaurants had opened and failed in that spot, I was confident. We were kind of out of the way inside the hotel and off the strip, but I figured people would find us because I was going to make sure we were hard to miss.

We started off with a bang, hosting a huge grand opening during the NBA's All-Star weekend with tons of sports stars and celebrities: Shaq, Fat Joe, Natalie Cole and Ludacris. The event was a huge success and it seemed like we were on our way.

On another level, things weren't so good.

The guys I had brought from Fort Lauderdale were starting to grow restless. I had made the move for me, yeah, but I also did it for these other guys, too. They were looking for a better life. Problem was, they all thought it was going to come overnight. In truth, I thought it might be a little like that, too. But I quickly realized Vegas was a different animal than South Florida, even though with the grand opening it had appeared we were going to have instant success. My guys either didn't figure that out or didn't want to face the fact that this wasn't going to be as easy as they thought. Then some of them started gambling, while others stayed up all hours of the night. They'd show up for work late, bitching and complaining. They were spending more than they were making and wanted more. Eventually they didn't show up at all.

After just four months in business at The Rio, I figured enough was enough and let the guys go. At a critical point, I found myself all alone in the restaurant wondering what I had done. I was flying back and forth between my home and Vegas, and though Café Martorano was doing great business, the stress was killing me.

No one really knew what I was going through. I was 1,500 miles from home trying to run a mom-and-pop operation against the big boys. The hotel couldn't really help me—we were just leasing space then—and I had just a handful of people I could count on. (One person in particular, who became a great friend, was always there for me and still is. I value that relationship.) Thank God, for them, but mostly I was alone. It was my ass on the line.

At night—every night—I couldn't sleep, but I was exhausted. I'd sit in my hotel room and stare out at the pool. I didn't regret my decision to let the guys go because, good or bad, I'd always shot from the hip; however, I did realize I'd made a tough job that much tougher. One evening after a hard day of work, I looked in the mirror and saw big, half-moon shadows under my eyes. I'd seen that look before, and it wasn't good. I turned on the TV and started to watch the movie "Rocky" with Sylvester Stallone.

"It ain't about how hard you hit," I listened to Rocky tell his son, "it's about how hard you can get hit and keep moving forward—how much you can take and keep moving forward. That's how winning is done."

The words spoke to me. They reminded me of everything I'd been through and all I wanted to accomplish. I watched the movie again and again, night after night for eight months. I knew it word for word.

It's kind of funny the way little things like that get you through the day, but stuff like watching Rocky Balboa and listening to Sam Cooke's "A Change Is Gonna Come" helped pull me up and face the next day. Every night that fucking place brought me to my knees—I never knew if I was going to be cooking for one or 1,000—but I took it day by day, punch by punch.

In September, I somehow managed to pull off another successful big event—Ludacris' 30th birthday party. It was a red-carpet thing, and, again, tons of celebrities came to Café Martorano: Robin Leach of "Lifestyles Of The Rich and Famous" TV show (he became a very dear and close friend of mine), Quincy Jones, Gabrielle Union, and Timbaland among many others. Ludacris had a gift made for 40 of his closest friends. It was a ring symbolizing friendship, and he gave me one. Things were looking up.

Mario Barth, the artist, the legend.

CHAPTER 41

About a month or so after the Ludacris party, I was doing some cardio work. In addition to lifting weights, I had made it my practice to take a 4-mile walk in the mornings. But halfway through my trip from the Rio to Madalay Bay, I felt a burning sensation on the right side of my upper chest that lasted a few seconds and went away. Fuck it, I thought.

The next day I did more cardio at the gym and experienced the same thing. I called my doctor, Sheldon Warman, in Fort Lauderdale, and made an appointment for a stress test as soon as I got off the plane. I was pressing a lot of weight—400 pounds—so I thought it might be a muscle pain. Still, I wanted my mind to be at ease for the big week ahead; I had a trip planned to New York City to talk with the Food Network about a possible show.

Two years earlier, I had had a stress test with Dr. Michael Chizner and everything was OK, so I figured that's where I was supposed to have the tests again. But when I showed up at the office, all the lights were off. I found one of the office nurses and explained the situation. Apparently, I had the wrong place, but Dr. Chizner, a friend, heard my voice and joined us. He was getting ready to leave for the weekend, but was concerned about the pain I was experiencing.

"I don't like the sound of that," he said. "I want to take a look—right away."

"But Doc," I said, "you don't understand. I've got a thing on Monday with the Food Network. I gotta catch a plane."

"I'll take a look and put a stent in you," he said. "You'll go home the next day and be able to fly to New York on Monday."

There was no use arguing. I was admitted to the hospital and Dr. Chizner went in for a look. When I woke up, the first thing I saw was his face, and he was shaking his head. Ninety-eight percent of three of the major arteries leading to my heart were clogged, including one called "The Widow-Maker."

"Chances are, if you would have gotten on that plane, you probably would have taken a nap and never got up," he said.

Just like my father, I thought.

Despite my condition, my mind never left Vegas. It was what I was talking about going into the operating room and afterward in the recovery room. I needed to get back there and make it work.

I had surgery and the doctor ordered me to stay at home and take it easy. No lifting weights. No Vegas. No stress. Five days after the operation, I got a surprise visit at my house from Lorraine Bracco. Even though I was in a lot of pain, I didn't want to show it. I insisted that she stay for dinner. She was polite and declined, but I put my foot down. Lorraine Bracco is in my house, I thought. Fuck this, I'm cooking. I convinced her to stay, and we had a nice light meal: past-and-peas and eggplant stack. That made me want to get back into the kitchen for good.

Macaroni and Peas

You can do this dish red or white—whatever you like. To serve it red, just skip the chicken stock at the end and add a can of San Marzano tomatoes.

>>> Dice half a white onion and saute it along with 3 cloves of smashed garlic in a pan with about 3 tablespoons of extra-virgin olive oil. Season the onion with a little Kosher salt and granulated garlic powder. When the onion is soft and the garlic is golden brown, add ½ cup of frozen peas and ½ cup of chicken stock. Simmer for 20 minutes. I like to serve this with tubetti, a small, tubular macaroni usually used in soups, but you can use whatever you like. Serve with some grated pecorino-romano and a pinch of hot pepper flakes.

Top: The Patron Saint Padre Pia, whose hands had the stigmata of Christ.

Bottom: I got this tattoo of Coleman Federal in honor of Cuz George who is doing life there for a non-violent crime.

For weeks I waded in the pool behind my home. I tried to make peace with my situation. If Vegas wasn't going to work, it wasn't going to work; I was still going to be a bigger success than had I stayed home in South Philly and drove a truck for John's Vending or shined shoes and sold soft pretzels. Part of me knew that. But a bigger part wanted to fight like Rocky. That's what I was, a fighter—and a fighter fights.

Against the doctor's orders, I had my sons go out and get me some light weights and I began working out in the pool. Little by little, I added weight and did some slow walking. Sooner than the doctors wanted, I got back to The Zoo, my gym, with the help of my trainer Louis "Angel" Evans, a great bodybuilder back in the day in Brooklyn. (He was a world-class champion. He's 66 now and in better shape than me. I couldn't have done it without his help and guidance.)

Just a few weeks after the surgery, I received a phone call from Dr. Warman while I was doing curls in the gym.

"How are you feeling, my boy?" he asked.

"I'm just taking it one day at a time."

I asked when I could return to work and start lifting weights again. He told me to continue to take it easy, but had no idea I was already in the gym against doctor's orders. (What can I say? I've got a hard Sicilian head.)

At that time, there were a lot of rumors we were going to close in Vegas. That never crossed my mind, but a few weeks after the operation, the Harrah's people approached me with a partnership deal that made my life a little easier. It was still going to be my food, my quality, my name—but I wasn't going to have to be there night in and night out. Plus, they believed in what I was doing; nothing was really going to change. I had always wanted to go up against the big dogs like Rao's, Emril and Batali. For me to be in the same ballpark against those guys was a great opportunity. I wasn't about to give that up. I wanted to keep fighting. It ain't about how hard you hit, cuz. It's about how hard you can get hit and keep moving forward.

Top: Steve visiting his cousin George Martorano in Coleman Federal. Picture taken by prison guard.

Middle: The Zoo, a serious workout gym in Fort Lauderdale.

Bottom: My trainer and close friend, Angel Evans.

CHAPTER 42

Three years have passed since that day I made the deal with the Harrah's people, and we're still standing. I haven't slowed down a bit. What else am I going to do? Drive a fucking truck? I think anyone else would have slowed down. But that's not me.

In fact, I'm busier than ever. I'm not a guy who likes to sit still. I've got a line of jarred sauces, along with my Chianti and Pinot Grigio wines. We opened a new restaurant at the Hard Rock Casino in Hollywood, Florida, with others on the way. I started an annual "Martorano's Masters Meatball Eating Contest" at the Rio in Vegas. I have an agent in New York, Jodi Turk, and a publicist in Florida, Alan Brown. I'm currently looking at TV and film opportunities —who knows?

It's funny. Sometimes I walk out of the Rio in Vegas while eating a fried meatball and look up at the billboard with my picture on it. I stop and wonder: Who would have ever thought that a meatball could get me to Vegas? Isn't that the same kid who used to cook chicken cutlets in his mother's basement? And then I laugh. Still is. Same guy. Still cooking like that. What am I going to do? Vacation in Italy? Retire?

Most guys in my line of work would do that, but not me. I still care. I'm still on the line every night cooking my fucking balls off. I'm not going to forget who I am or where I came from.

I can't.

I'm like that meatball of mine: big, bold and South Philly all the way. My life, My Food, My way. YO CUZZZ!

The Grand Opening Celebration—Seminole Hard Rock Hotel & Casino, Hollywood, Florida. The Mummers* traveled from South Philly to pay hommage to their favorate son, Steve Martorano.

*In full costume from the traditional New Year's celebration.

Steve at his Martorano's Meatball eating contest with the winner of the first two years—Joey "Jaws" Chestnut. Held annually in Martorano's at the Rio, Las Vegas.

Rio
NOW OPEN!
ITALIAN YOU CAN'T RESIST.
Martorano's

THANK YOU TO THE GREAT PATRONS OF CAFÈ MARTORANO.

1. Archie Manning, Steve Martorano and Peyton Manning **2.** Baby Face, Gabrielle Union and Chris Tucker **3.** David Proval **4.** Lorraine Bracco, Steve and Danny DeVito **5.** Gabrielle Union **6.** Nando **7.** Shane Mosley and Tom Jones **8.** Tom Cruise **9.** Jimmy Kimmel **10.** Steve and Eddie Jones **11.** Fat Joe **12.** Frankie Vincent **13.** Jeremy Roenik and wife, Tracy **14.** Cool **15.** Charles and Rhonda Johnson **16.** Micky Arison. **17.** Joe Montana **18.** Joseph R. Gannascoli. **19.** Kim Kardashian, Steve and Reggie Bush **20.** Ludacris and Steve **21.** Michael Imperioli

IT HAS BEEN A REAL JOY.

22.

23.

24.

25.

26.

27.

28.

29.

30.

31.

32.

33.

34.

35.

36.

37.

22. Cuz Mike Cappola, Henry Pisano, Sonny Ciferni, Michael Baldino, Steve **23.** Rick Pitino and Steve Martorano **24.** Shaq and Steve on New Years Eve **25.** Chazz Palmi **26.** Jamie Foxx **27.** Steve and Natalie Cole **28.** Scott Storch **29.** Steve and Vincent Pastore **30.** Steve and Ludacris **31.** Cuz George from Jimmy Kimmel **32.** Steve Martorano, Steve Stowe and Shaq **33.** Zach and Steve in Las Vegas **34.** Steve and Robin Leach **35.** Ice-T and Coco **36.** Jerry Blavat, DJ **37.** Arthur J. Nascarella

RECIPE INDEX MARTORANO